BARBARIC SPORT

BARBARIC SPORT

A GLOBAL PLAGUE

MARC PERELMAN
Translated by John Howe

VERSO
London • New York

Liberté · Égalité · Fraternité
RÉPUBLIQUE FRANÇAISE

This book is supported by the Institut français as part of the Burgess Programme.
(www.frenchbooknews.com).

This edition first published by Verso 2012
© Verso 2012
Translation © John Howe
First published as *Le sport barbare. Critique d'un fléau mondial*
© Editions Michalon, Paris 2011
The 'Twenty Theses on Sport' ('Vingt thèses sur le sport') were published in the
first issue of the review *Quel corps?* (April 1975). They have been republished twice:
in Jean-Marie Brohm's *Critiques du sport* (1976); then, in an altered form, in an
anthology entitled *L'Opium sportif*, edited by Jean-Pierre Escriva and
Henri Vaugrand (1996); the theses first appeared in English in Jean-Marie Brohm,
Sport: A Prison of Measured Time, London: Pluto Press, 1987

1 3 5 7 9 10 8 6 4 2

Verso
UK: 6 Meard Street, London W1F 0EG
US: 20 Jay Street, Suite 1010, Brooklyn, NY 11201
www.versobooks.com

Verso is the imprint of New Left Books

ISBN-13: 978-1-84467-859-4

British Library Cataloguing in Publication Data
A catalogue record for this book is available from the British Library

Library of Congress Cataloging-in-Publication Data
Perelman, Marc.
[Sport barbare. English]
Barbaric sport : a global plague / Marc Perelman ;
translated by John Howe.
p. cm.
Includes bibliographical references.
Translated from French.
ISBN 978-1-84467-859-4 -- ISBN 978-1-84467-913-3
1. Sports and state. 2. Sports--Sociological aspects.
3. Sports--Corrupt practices. 4. Sports and
globalization. I. Title.
GV706.35.P47513 2012
306.483--dc23

2012003763

Typeset in Bembo by MJ Gavan, Cornwall, UK
Printed and bound by CPI Group (UK) Ltd, Croydon, CR0 4YY

We know that modern education makes great use of sports to distract the young from sexual activity: it would be more accurate to say that it replaces specifically sexual pleasure with that provided by movement, and that it relegates sexual activity to one of the auto-erotic components.
Sigmund Freud, *Three Essays on the Theory of Sexuality*

In a period henceforth marked by sport, men know at last what they have to do. Everywhere balls can be seen whizzing through the air …
For the sake of the masses, they have built stadiums …
Sport makes the masses stupid.
Siegfried Kracauer, *Le Voyage et la danse*

The Olympic Games are reactionary.
Walter Benjamin, Écrits français

There is no apolitical sport.
Ernst Bloch, *The Hope Principle*

Sporting events were the models for totalitarian mass rallies …
Sport corresponds to the predatory, aggressive and practical spirit …
Sport implies not only the desire to do violence, but also to undergo it oneself, to suffer.
Theodor W. Adorno, *Prisms*

The more leisure activities diversify, museum, football or Adriatic cruise, the more standardized the participants become.
Max Horkheimer, *Critical Notes (1949–1969)*

In the yelling at sports events there is already a 'murderous' resonance.
Günther Anders, *Human Obsolescence*

CONTENTS

PREFACE

This essay aims to show that the powerful globalization process now under way, driven by a plundering financial capitalism – which also controls all the trade on the planet and is starting to dismember it as a planet – has been put to use, indeed taken over and given direction, by a deep-rooted social phenomenon whose main lines of force and extensive sphere of influence we would like to expose. This extraordinary phenomenon weighs heavily, exercising an ever-increasing negative pressure, on the very possibility of making sense of a society that has become opaque to itself while shaping reality in its own image. But that is not the essential point. The phenomenon we are going to describe in terms of its most salient (but often also most invisible) characteristics pertains more importantly to a *colonization of the body* in many of those who devote themselves to it relentlessly, and a *mutilation of awareness* in all those mesmerized by it as a spectacle.

To put it another way, this global phenomenon plays a leading part in a new form of barbarism into which whole swathes of Western, Asian and Middle Eastern societies have collapsed … This recent form of barbarism (in the sense of strangeness, rudeness, vulgarity, ignorance and cruelty) threatens in our view the literal destruction of most of the values and ideals inherent to post-Enlightenment society but overturned by today's lethal modernity (whether or not we slap a postmodern label on it). The state of ruin and gloomy disorder that blights the whole of society affects individuals first of all, encroaching on their actual existence, modifying their very essence as living beings possessing a body and a consciousness. The phenomenon in question is largely responsible for the barbaric society to which we are subjected, unable as we are to devise any real form of resistance to its violence.

An unequalled social, political and ideological power has thus developed with extraordinary speed, spreading across the planet like a pandemic, sweeping away all that still remained in modern societies of opportunities for play, bodily freedom, simple pleasure in movement, and more broadly the idea of an open, living culture with a flourishing vernacular aspect. Ideals and projects of emancipation, of solidarity, of creation, have been turned into their opposites, almost cancelled out, by that phenomenon that arose in Europe at the end of the nineteenth century and spread across the world in the short century that followed.

The everyday lives of billions of individuals are thus contaminated, consumed, infected by its constant assaults, its capacity for insidious infiltration, its innocent-seeming mischief. More worryingly, people have become accustomed to it, so that its existence has become part of our daily lives; and this almost invisibly, because the degree and scale of its invasion (of all space) and its occupation (of all time) are such that we can no longer see it, because we see nothing else.

We have just described, in the broadest of strokes, what is usually designated by the term 'sport'.

1. THE REAL NATURE OF THE OLYMPIC GAMES: BERLIN 1936, MOSCOW 1980. THE FOOTBALL WORLD CUP, ARGENTINA 1978

We were warned a long time ago by the philosopher Vladimir Jankélévitch, whose experience of Nazi Germany taught him that

> it is advisable to be reserved on the youth myth when it is linked with exaltation of strength. The *Jugendbewegung* was born in Germany along with its pseudo-metaphysics; it developed in the Hitler Youth and has invisibly contaminated democratic youth movements, socialist sport and the 'Olympic spirit', all of which have unguardedly aped the Nuremberg style with its monstrous liturgies. Nazi juvenilism rests entirely on the sacralization of brute strength and intoxicating pagan vitality … Make no mistake: exaltation of the youthful body is in many cases a suspect myth fabricated by the triumphant male's prestige. Beware of beautiful athletes.

At the end of the Berlin Olympics, in *Le Journal* of 27 August 1936, the founder of the IOC, Baron Pierre de Coubertin defended the event in these terms:

> What! The Games disfigured, the Olympic Idea sacrificed to propaganda? That's completely wrong! The grandiose success of the Berlin Games served the Olympic ideal magnificently. … The Olympic Idea must be allowed to blossom freely, without fear of the passion and excess which create the necessary excitement and enthusiasm. … People are worried in France by the fact that the 1936 Games were illuminated by Hitlerite strength and discipline.

How could it have been otherwise? On the contrary, it is eminently desirable for the Games to be thus clothed, with the same success, in the garment woven for them over four years by each people.

All through the period of Hitler's dictatorship, sport was one of the main vectors for propagating Nazi ideology, and rapidly became a veritable social and political plague afflicting a population in thrall to totalitarian order. In August 1936, three and a half years after Hitler's accession to power, the Berlin Olympic Games and their grandiose production, both inside the stadium and outside it in the city itself, revealed the real function of sport in a totalitarian society. The Games demonstrated that sport played a key part in a militarized system that was persecuting intellectuals, brutalizing Jews before trying to exterminate them, and preparing to mobilize the youth for a future war of conquest across Europe.

Contrary to what used to be thought (and is still thought today, whether through naivety or simple ignorance), the 1936 Olympic Games in Berlin – a priori a neutral, innocent, pure and spotless sporting event – were not instrumentalized by the Nazi government; they were not taken over or appropriated by Nazi policy. Instead the Games by nature simply were an effective instrument, an efficient tool, a great practical apparatus for pursuing racist, anti-Semitic and repressive policies against domestic opponents of the regime, just as they were one of the main vectors of an intense phase of preparation for the Second World War which began three years later.

The Nazi aediles and Hitler himself, initially sceptical about the political advantages of such an event, but courted by the International Olympic Committee from 1931 and the end of the Weimar Republic, were able to rely on the IOC's support throughout the competition. The preparation as well as the conduct of the Berlin Olympics provided cover for the intensified activities of the Hitlerite state, helping to conceal its decision to invade neighbouring countries and, inside Germany, to justify redoubling the violent repression of those opposed to the regime that had been developing since 1933, especially trade unionists, communists and Jews.

The IOC kept its gaze averted from such matters before, during and after the Games, even though the current Olympic Charter, dating from 1933, seemed – albeit in rather cumbersome terms

– to be calling for beneficial encounters between peoples and individuals:

> [The reviver of the Olympic Games, as well as his first collaborators] thought quite rightly that those gatherings of young men were one of the best ways to make the different classes in a country as well as units of different civilizations well acquainted with each other and to promote better understanding. Those who followed did their utmost to improve that wonderful manifestation, which is the sporting criterion of the races of the world, and contributed worthily to bring together those who have taken part in the Games.

The swastika flag and the five-ringed Olympic flag thus flew side by side during the 'festival of youth', and together decorated the main streets of the new Reich's cities. The linking of the two flags helped immeasurably to mask the sinister reality of Nazi power and hide the triumph of a declared policy of aggression, conjuring out of sight its wish to enslave non-Aryan peoples and its schemes for their programmed destruction – all the fevered groundwork for the barbaric state's future crimes.

That screen, that curtain of dreamy well-being, the affecting imagery of exulting masses intoxicated by the sporting spectacle of the Berlin Olympic Games, thus served to cloak a much darker reality already horribly at work in Germany. The 1936 Olympics did not mark a period of peace, nor did they make one more likely, even though many individuals were spellbound by the near-perfect organization that delivered such a colossal, magical spectacle. On the contrary, the 1936 Games enabled the Nazis to fettle their weapons unmolested, despite numerous calls for a boycott including some from the US. It seemed this sporting festival for the world's youth, with added art and culture, really had become what Baron Pierre de Coubertin called it a year earlier: the new 'religion' of the 'philosophic foundations of modern Olympism', in which 'the modern athlete exalts his fatherland, his race, his flag'. During the festival – *with* the festival, perhaps – a vast project was taking shape, one that led to world catastrophe.

Forty-four years later in 1980, the power of the Moscow Olympics helped for the whole period of the Games to dissimulate the existence of labour camps and psychiatric asylums on Soviet territory. The Games had also been used to justify the invasion of Afghanistan by Red Army tanks the previous year.

Two years before that, in 1978, the football World Cup held in Argentina had enabled the blood-stained Videla dictatorship to establish itself by crushing all dissent, smashing all opposition, arresting people en masse and cutting up opponents with chainsaws 300 yards from the River Plate stadium in Buenos Aires. The roaring of the crowds in the stadium drowned the screams of the tortured; local fans, their awareness and conscience mutilated by football, fervently applauded their national team which finally emerged victorious, giving the dictatorship a further boost. Football, that modern emotional plague, was doing its job.

There are other examples. A few days before the 1968 Olympics in Mexico came the massacre of several hundred students in Three Cultures Square, organized with astonishing cynicism by the government of the time. When members of the Israeli team were murdered during the 1972 Munich Olympics, the IOC president Avery Brundage (1952–72) – a former Nazi sympathizer and member of the isolationist and xenophobic America First Committee – said famously that 'The Games must go on'.

But those three major events – the Berlin and Moscow Olympics, and the World Cup held in Argentina – remain outstanding for the determining socio-political place occupied by sport, not as an annexe to the internal political situation but, on the contrary, playing a fundamental role in the advent and consolidation of the regimes and governments in question, and of the institutions and individuals associated with them. The more recent example of the 2008 Beijing Olympics is a perfect case in point.

2. BEIJING 2008:
THE GAMES OF SHAME

The 2008 Beijing Olympics were not all that different from the 1980 Moscow Olympics, and quite similar to the 1936 Berlin ones. They were framed in the same way as those Games by an omnipresent police force and army hunting down dissidents, itinerant workers, trade unionists, beggars, prostitutes and riff-raff. The strident nationalist mobilization of the masses, the party's will to impose permanent control and the generalized stupidity were as striking as they were in 1936 Berlin.

More importantly, the major themes being developed by China and its President Hu Jintao shared some of the ideological elements of Olympism as set out in the Olympic Charter. Since 2006, the diplomatic and political reorganization of China had sought to open up the country against a background of reformist policies. Three insistent themes recurred: lasting peace, common prosperity and a harmonious world. In China's view, the idea of a harmonious world should be judged by its willingness to question the hegemony of the great powers, especially the US, to remedy North–South contradictions or to deal with the environmental crisis. Chinese leaders seized every opportunity to make speeches rehashing the same arguments: we must all struggle for peace, seek peaceful solutions, avoid resorting to military force or sanctions. 'Harmonious coexistence' between the US and China replaced the former 'peaceful coexistence' between the US and the USSR. To better understand the current political thematics in China, it is helpful to compare them with Olympian thematics, in particular the ones contained in the Olympic Charter.

Thus, when the Olympic Games are described as the 'youth festival of the entire world', it is profitable to be able to read between the lines. The Beijing Games exhibited from the outset a large deployment of police and security forces. China had announced that

> a total of 80,000 persons, including police officers, professional security agents and volunteers will be deployed as protection for the 29th Olympic Games which will take place in Beijing in August 2008. ... 'Beijing is making every effort to establish a high-quality professional security force for Chinese and foreign participants in the Beijing Olympic Games,' said Ma Zhenchuan, director of the Municipal Bureau of Public Security, on Monday during a conference on international cooperation to ensure security at the Beijing Olympic Games. A set of special manuals, comprising seventeen categories and totalling 180,000 characters, has been prepared for training purposes, covering elementary knowledge of the Olympic Games, essential words and expressions for security personnel, international decorum and courtesy, basic knowledge of the religions, customs and conventions of different peoples, and first aid. So far, 25,000 persons have completed training courses for this purpose. According to Liu Jing, vice-minister of public security, the department of security for the Beijing Olympic Games has established fifty-two General Security Plans, counting those for the gymnasiums and stadiums. (chine-informations.com)

This comprehensive coverage of public space by police and troops was not really a novelty when any Olympic Games were installed in the city designated by the IOC. What was new in this case was the fact that the Chinese police were themselves under close surveillance. China had launched a campaign to 'improve the image' of police officers in Beijing and other cities involved in the Games, the official media reported. In particular, officers were forbidden to smoke, eat or converse among themselves while on duty. Policemen would be supervised by 'inspectors' in uniform and plain clothes 'to see how they behave when people ask for their help', the sources said, citing police ministry spokesman Wu Heping. Any citizen who spotted a policeman smoking, eating or chatting while on duty should 'report' them by telephoning 110, added Jia Chunming, a senior Beijing police official.

The campaign was being launched in the six cities where the 2008 Games would be held – Beijing, Shanghai, Qingdao, Shenyang, Tianjin and Qinhuangdao – and would be extended to a number of major tourist sites at the beginning of 2008, the official sources said. In June, a directive had banned police officers from wearing 'scarves, jewellery, beards or strangely dyed hair', Reuters reported in September 2007. And all that was only the foundation of the comprehensive strengthening of security: part of the population of Beijing was also to be mobilized, to back up police perhaps thought deficient or not sufficiently numerous. Who better to supervise the people than the people themselves! 'More than 600,000 Beijing residents are to be asked to supplement the security forces during the 2008 Olympic Games,' AFP reported on 9 March 2007. 'During the Games, security professionals will not be acting alone. They will have the support of several hundred thousand volunteers and fans,' according to the deputy secretary of the Beijing Communist Party, Qiang Wei, quoted by the daily *Beijing News*. He added that 100,000 police officers, in addition to other security professionals, would be on duty from 8 to 24 August 2008 to eliminate any risk of trouble during the Games. Berlin 1936 and Moscow 1980 had found a worthy successor.

The IOC, as represented by its current president, Jacques Rogge, was equally up to speed on events linked to the Games, especially those sited in Tibet. Having maintained a shameful silence throughout the worst of the repression there, Rogge dismissed calls for a boycott of the Games from human-rights campaigners, saying he believed China 'would change' as a result of organizing the Games:

'The Olympic Games are a force for good. They are a catalyst for change, not a cure for all ills,' affirmed a press release distributed in Olympia, Greece, where the Olympic Flame is scheduled to be ignited next Monday. 'The IOC is respectful of human rights. We respect NGOs and campaigning groups, as well as the causes they support – and we also hold regular talks with them – but we are neither a political organization nor a campaigning organization,' Jacques Rogge explained. (*Le Monde*, 23 March 2008.)

With the IOC, Count Rogge organized the Beijing Games in close cooperation with the Chinese Organizing Committee, itself under the thumb of the Party-State. The president of the French National Olympic and Sporting Committee (CNOSF), Henri Sérandour, had been given a three-month suspended prison sentence and fined 20,000 euros in October 2006 for 'prise illégale d'intérêt' – unlawful conflict of interest in a public official – and 'reprimanded' by the IOC in December 2007, just days before the end of his mandate. But as in the capitals of other nations to be visited by the Olympic flame, in Paris daily meetings were held with Chinese Embassy officials ... presided by Sérandour. With the IOC and China making common cause over all else, defence of the Games meant trampling the Tibetans underfoot by ignoring the violent repression they suffered, involving many deaths and a thousand campaigners in jail.

That, in turn, made it impossible for the IOC to escape implication in the Tibetan repression. After all, it was surely no more coerced by the Chinese dictatorship than the dictatorship was coerced by the Olympic Games. On the contrary, the IOC and the Chinese Party-State, convinced of their common interests, together did their utmost to ensure that these Games would have the grand scale of a planetary sporting spectacle. For the Chinese dictatorship, that meant relying totally for the mounting of the Games on inputs from the IOC and its national committees. Since 1984 or even earlier, China had understood that the Olympic Games were a vast sporting/commercial enterprise able to concentrate the attention of all nations; and that it could act through the IOC and its national committees to assert its own viewpoint as a dictatorial great power, thus ensuring acquiescence in its acts of internal repression and terror.

'URBAN REGENERATION': THE ROLE OF THE OLYMPICS

The run-up to the Olympic Games saw an acceleration of the vast campaign of demolition in the old city, the radical extirpation of its historic kernel. The brand-new, instant, cultural (and above all sporting) Beijing represented a bald denial of the city's history: the gnarled human-scale palimpsest of millennia had been briskly erased and replaced with gigantic, Western-style towers and slabs. The

Olympics played a direct role in the destructive climax of a razing of the urban landscape begun in the 1950s and amplified some years later by the Deng Xiaoping regime. The city had always been the very arena of history, and its centre concentrated the essences of liberty and tyranny alike. Perhaps more the latter since, to quote Karl Marx, society has always tended to 'subordinate the country-side to the town'; but the current tendency of the Chinese city is self-liquidation in a disquietingly overheated economy, involving the insistent display of its chosen face and a mushrooming of gigantic urban objects planted as close as possible to its heart.

The grandiose engineering and architectural achievements represented by stadiums, swimming pools and gymnasiums, as well as the offices of mass communications (the new TV centre designed by Rem Koolhaas) or culture (the Opera House by Paul Andreu) together contaminate the fabric of Beijing, spreading like a stain, driven by the new economic policy: a ravening, all-devouring capitalism running at record speed. Most of the sports structures were built to far tighter deadlines than is usual for that sort of architecture, and consequently under very harsh working conditions. The work had to be ready on time. The flat-out rhythm of these immense building sites bristling with cranes even started to worry IOC aediles accustomed to hard competition. '"The Chinese were so far ahead that for the first time in its history, the IOC had to ask a city hosting the Games to slow down a bit," says Kevan Gosper, a senior spokesman of the IOC's Press Commission' (*Sport*, No. 163, 8 February 2008).

In the space of a few years China's cities had exploded out of their historic boundaries, with their population steadily increasing. The incomers swelling the cities came essentially from the countryside as the result of unprecedented urban drift. And these new urban populations, propelled from the rural depths towards what were often new towns, were taking possession of territory in a new urban landscape decreed by a celestial bureaucracy, but under social and especially environmental conditions that were completely unknown to them. A segment of this former peasantry, deployed in the first instance in immense building sites to meet the challenge of building and then inhabiting the new cities, constitutes the new urban battalions whose members still lack awareness of the vast movement of historical change that carries them forward.

Freshly arrived in mushrooming cities, this barely urbanized peasantry had consented, in order to survive, to be dumped in a wasteland where nothing had yet happened and nothing was ever going to happen, apart from the more or less immediate prospect of the Olympic Games. There the new city-dwellers, so recently wrenched from their native settings, tried to establish a life. Free at last of the traditional forms that still enslaved them in the country-side, they were now stacked in apartments inside blocks surrounded by other apartments and identical blocks … 'The forces of historical absence are starting to compose their own exclusive landscape.' Filed among endless stacks of concrete shelves, similar to France's lifeless new suburbs but on a far larger scale and in far greater numbers, the transplanted peasant masses inhabit a world where architectural objects, and in particular purpose-built sporting venues, constitute the city's new poles of attraction, its magnetic poles, the visible signs of a Beijing making its violent and precipitate entry into the twenty-first century. In an endless landscape of massive rectangular slabs of housing, often of identical design, only these sporting edifices, and a few scattered cultural venues, testified to the outside world that a real renovation had taken place in the Chinese capital. In effect, the hasty development of Beijing and the other Olympic cities in prepara-tion for the Games was pivoted and focused on the sporting venues, whose stadiums were to be the visible signs, the tangible proofs, of China's great vitality.

Beijing, millennial capital of the Middle Kingdom, seat of all the central organisms of the Chinese Communist Party, now intended to become a world city: a total capital. To this end the Beijing Olympic Games served as a decisive launch pad, a vector accelerating the pro-cesses of demolition and reconstruction, already well advanced, to an unprecedented paroxysm of speed. Beijing's role as a political capital had been endorsed by the IOC's decision in July 2001 to give the Games to the awakening economic giant's flagship city. By placing such trust in its executives, the IOC had effectively backed Beijing's claim to be a political capital and a model of urban development for the rest of the world.

THE SPORTING FACE OF THE NEW BEIJING

Imposing, gigantic and gigantist, colossal, monumental; the collusive leavening of the grim, dehumanized architecture of ferroconcrete modernity with a scattering of 'new' forms associating plastic, metal and glass in iridescent and sometimes garish colours … Such is the chaotic urban regeneration, the immoderate architecture, of the world's most powerful dictatorship. Olympic Beijing was the setting for visual and auditory shock and awe, sparked off its vast and soulless urban architecture by the steel of immeasurable political power, wielded by new emperors who rule more than a billion individual subjects, seventeen million of them in the city of Beijing alone. For mass urban renovation and architectural kudos were central components in the new image China and Beijing wanted to project to the world, which was duly subjected to them non-stop, twenty-four hours a day, for the fifteen days of the competition.

On this immeasurable scale, urban redevelopment and its architecture cannot be seen merely as the reflection of a society perhaps unused to them, but welcoming them all the same; they are not just the 'mirror' to a society in the process of transformation. On the contrary, architecture and urban renewal are a stated priority of Chinese society, the wilful materialization on its own territory of a whole conception of the existence and dynamic – the future – of society. The architecture and the resulting cityscape are de facto participants in a *project*, anticipating something, conceiving it and in the end achieving it, a plan embracing a new assemblage of lifestyles, modes of travel, ways of working: a new set of real living conditions.

So, architecture and urban renewal are not neutral endeavours, independent of the social context; they are decreed and conceived in the repositories of political and of course economic executive power. And they embody aesthetic, sociological, scientific and technological standards. They create or recreate a primarily visual meaning whose outlines, shapes, materials and overall style may sometimes jostle secular attitudes. Urban regeneration and its architecture found an original, all-new space populated by static, forceful, everlasting structures. And in turn those sharply-hewn, definitive shapes favour a certain view of the world, establish a relation to the world mediated through such forms.

As soon as the IOC decided to give the Games to Beijing, in July 2001, the city was subjected to a profound upheaval, radical in every way, affecting the very structure of the city, its organization, its disposition, its statutes. More generally, in Beijing as in other cities hosting recent Olympic Games (Montreal, Seoul, Athens), it seems that architecture and urban renewal contribute to a new orientation in the context of the current globalization process: the homogenization and unification of all cities. So it is no small thing to see a great and ancient city like Beijing, marked by the fine-grained primal history of its architecture and a unique urban lifestyle, taking a violent, definitive swerve in a completely different direction, developing a spatial tendency generated by the scrawls of trendy urban architects; bowing, in a word, to the diktat of megalomaniac mediocrities in quest of recognition.

But the present regeneration of Beijing does not dismiss the idea that the city taking shape might have some historical and aesthetic value in the future. The demolition of elements from the past – the heritage of bricks and mortar, traditional construction – just shows how little they were valued following the decision to hold the Games in Beijing. An aesthetic value or valuation is always included, or superimposed, on the historical value of a city. The problem that arises is precisely the aesthetic value of the city, Beijing in this case, as a new visual space. What will become of Beijing and the other Olympic towns after the wave of sporting construction, swimming pools, stadiums, gymnasiums, velodromes has passed … not forgetting the consequences in terms of roads? What will become of Beijing which, in just a few years, has suffered the direct and irreversible shock of redevelopment sweeping away the old city? What is Beijing becoming, now that almost its entire area, outside the Forbidden City, has been remodelled in the totalitarian manner: in the furnace of urban renewal at gunpoint, with the destruction of everything old, anything that might get in the way of the bulldozers, and the creation of immense avenues leading to monumental buildings devoted to sport?

With a historical symmetry at once satisfying and disturbing, the master planner of Beijing's radical overhaul was the son and namesake of Adolf Hitler's architect and later minister of armaments and munitions, Albert Speer – described modestly in his son's official CV as a 'politician'. Aspects of the plan caused controversy from the start, in particular a twenty-six-kilometre boulevard linking the Olympic Park with Tiananmen Square in the centre of Beijing:

> It is on this boulevard … that the polemic is centred. The boulevard and especially its conceiver are criticized in effect as being inspired by the plans for Berlin drawn up by Hitler's architect Albert Speer. You may say that there is nothing surprising there, given that the said 'conceiver' is none other than Albert Speer Jr., the controversial architect's son.
>
> Burdened by the oppressive heritage of his father, Albert Speer Jr. survived this polemic only through the support of the Olympic Committee, affirming that the plan in question conformed to the city of Beijing's desired and accepted vision for the lay-out and development of the city. (aroots.org, 18 February 2003.)

When it comes to Olympism and sporting constructions on a very large scale, the past catches up with the present or even overtakes it. The comparison of 1936 Berlin with 2008 Beijing does not seem unreasonable. Back in the 1930s, Albert Speer was in charge of Berlin's urban renovation and of building the city's stadium. Seventy years on, Speer's offspring revived his approach, arranging the city of Beijing around the magnetic poles of numerous sports edifices and constructing an immense central axis that required the forced displacement of more than a million people. In both cases the IOC gave its full support to monumental architecture and urban redevelopment based on massive demolition and construction, without giving much thought to the displaced populations, let alone to the quality of the proposed buildings. As with Berlin in 1936, the new face of Beijing was hinged on a single value: its sporting value.

> The new emperors have lengthened the historic prospect, in what they see as a consecration. To the north, the building site for the Games is six times larger than the one in Athens, the time schedule far more advanced. The budget, some 35 million euros, is the biggest in history. To the thirty-seven stadiums – fourteen of them brand new – that will accommodate the Games, add a tripling of the underground railway system, a tangle of urban freeways and an international airport inspired by a dragon's sinuous back. The bulk of the work will be completed by the end of the year … 'We want

to show China's progress to the world,' declared Liu Qi, president of the Organizing Committee and leader of the Communist Party in Beijing. (*Le Figaro*, 4 April 2007.)

CELEBRITY ARCHITECTS

Thanks to the efforts of world-famous architects – Holland's Rem Koolhaas (who designed the headquarters of the state television channel CCTV), the Frenchman Paul Andreu (the Opera House), the Briton Norman Foster (the new international airport), the Swiss partnership of Meuron and Herzog (the Olympic stadium nicknamed the 'Bird's Nest') and the civil engineering group Ove Arup (the water-sports centre known to Beijing residents as the 'Ice Cube'), Beijing became the world's leading building site, but also the city that had appointed these star celebrities to bulldoze and recon-struct vast areas of its fabric before delivering them into the hands of opportunist speculators: housing had been opened up to private ownership under a law passed on 7 March 2004.

But the Olympic Games were to be the display window for the Chinese economic 'miracle'. The thirty-seven stadiums, fourteen of them brand new, were accompanied by a cat's cradle of freeways chopping up the city and its approaches and by an officially esti-mated 10,000 building sites. Suddenly, the slogan 'New Olympiads! A New Beijing!' made literal sense. Under the forceful guidance of the CCP and the IOC combined, Beijing saw an amplification of the transformation of its general physiognomy. The changes were aesthetic, certainly, but also transformed the urban structure and way of life, with the 'death sentence on the hutongs' and the dis-appearance too of the 'siheyuan, square courtyards with turned-up gables that gave charm to the imperial city' (*Le Figaro*, January 2008). Beijing in consequence had been for several years a gigantic pre-Olympics building site, swarming with hundreds of thousands of workers. But given the inordinate scale, most of the people working long hours were not traditional building labourers.

The Beijing building sites employ about half the mingong, migrant workers estimated to number around four million; perhaps two million workers are being employed to redraw the capital. Most come from the countryside, without papers, with no real rights or work contracts, and they regard themselves as 'relatively' better off working on these sites. No records are kept however of accidents or deaths, which are noticed only when fortuitously discovered by the press. ... The mingong are not a recent phenomenon, but their numbers have increased and they are today serving a Futurist architecture. The techniques used on the sites are sometimes reminiscent of traditional methods, but applied on the scale of the skyscraper, leaving a landscape like a Normandy beach on the morning after the Longest Day: jumbles of reinforcing bars and concrete blocks, unprotected holes and pitfalls, rusty girders, planks, nails, abandoned sheets of plywood ... The Olympic sites benefited from the experience of Paul Andreu while the big National Theatre (Opera House) was being constructed, a prolonged operation lasting from 2003 to 2008. It had involved shipping in the biggest crane in Germany, the first of its kind ever seen in China. The spidery crane was then surrounded by tens of thousands of workers during the most intense periods of construction, as if any machines, any tools of intermediate size were still inconceivable. ... Beijing, the biggest building site in history, is progressing in giant strides, but as the time for the Games (8 to 24 August) draws closer the jumpiness of the representatives of law and order is becoming ever more noticeable. The residents, like tourists and professional photographers, are especially wary of the private militias paid (poorly) by promoters and firms. The area around the big Qianmen site, south of Tiananmen Square and next to the desert left by the blossoming of the Opera House, is among the most dangerous in this respect, although it is also highly visible to the beleaguered defenders of what remains of old Beijing. ... The quarrel of the Ancients and the Moderns is raging in the wings. Will the 'identical' reconstruction of the vanished Beijing be the most urgent post-2008 priority? (*Le Monde*, 8 March 2008.)

Despite a historical error – 'Futurist' architecture was part of an Italian artistic movement current in the 1920s – the *Le Monde* piece, by Frédéric Edelmann who is very knowledgeable, appreciative and adept where colossal structures are concerned, did not hide a real concern at the spectacle of architecture and its mode of construction on such a shameless megalomaniac scale. For a start, it was the very immensity of the tasks imposed by the Games that called for the recruitment of an army of underpaid workers from a class liable to forced labour: the Games drove into development and employment a huge mass of sub-proletarians directly and exclusively used in the multiple Olympic sites. The article went on to show that Beijing had sought to redraw its image as a city by means of the Games: Beijing is literally an Olympic city.

The momentum generated by this vast wave of architectural projects and the construction of such numbers of ultramodern buildings carried urban planning along with it, to reshape all the districts of Beijing in the space of a few years. The generally low profile of the historic city, with one- and two-storey buildings being most typical of traditional Beijing architecture, was succeeded very rapidly by a tall vertical architecture of big, garishly coloured, sometimes flashy objects, essentially and violently anti-vernacular: an imported architecture. The low, uneven roofscapes of old Beijing vanished almost overnight under a mushrooming profusion of skyscrapers, under the pressure of a great flood of sports equipment awaiting the assault of the masses.

3. THE OLYMPIC CHARTER

I continue to regard as excellent the constitution of the IOC based on what I will call the principle of reverse delegation, meaning that the mandate starts from the Idea to generate disciples and not from the mass of disunited adherents to generate the Idea: a principle that could be applied in many domains and might contain, if not the salvation of contemporary society, at least a strong attenuation of its evils.

That quotation lays out in black and white what it is that rules the specifically anti-democratic principle built into the Olympic Games from its first origin, which persists to this day. The same IOC was awarded the status of observer in the United Nations on 19 October 2009, for its contribution to various initiatives in such areas as humanitarian aid, peace, education, gender equality, the environment and the struggle against HIV/AIDS. The IOC president Jacques Rogge declared on that occasion that 'this observer status is a major recognition of the role sport can play in building a peaceful and better world … Olympic values are in perfect agreement with the philosophy of the UN'.

Everyone effusively concurs, everyone asserts their agreement and presents or parades those values as a precious inheritance of all humanity. What is more, everyone would like to see them applied in all their rigour across the whole extent of the vast organization the charter controls from edge to edge of the Olympic territory: the entire planet. Sportsmen and women, sporting managers, politicians of every stripe, generally ignorant journalists: all refer to it with deep admiration, constantly exalt its memory, treat it almost as a cult object, a sort of fetish. Over the hundred years of its existence the Olympic Charter has become a text more than a hundred pages long, in its current downloadable version from the IOC website.

Five chapters and very numerous sub-sections, fattened with a collection of application texts expanding on rules, have weighted down the charter since its very first, light and thin incarnation, a century ago in 1908, published in French under the title *Annuaire* (almanac, year-book). The charter lengthened continuously over the years from the 1908 '*Règlement*' – rules and regulations – of barely two pages to become a 108-page book. It has become as it were a sacred text, the Bible of the Olympic movement, its legitimate and legitimizing armature. It enshrines a collection of rules which cannot be changed or repealed in part; it presents a list of rights and, especially, obligations. The Olympic Charter is the codification of Olympism. Its current edition is dated 11 February 2010.

The first official charter of the Olympic Games appeared in 1938; in 1949, thirteen years after the Nazi Games in Berlin and the year of its first publication under the title of 'Olympic Charter', there appeared the famous article specifying that 'Any form of discrimination with regard to a country or a person on grounds of race, religion or politics is incompatible with belonging to the Olympic Movement'. The Olympic Charter is both landmark and boundary of the Olympic Movement, defining with great precision its rights and its duties and marking out its history. It has become a legend, a sort of myth, because it serves as a base for all interpretations, commentaries and criticisms. It is mythical primarily because it is the *idealized representation* of an unchanging and essentially sporting humanity. According to the Olympic Charter, the main activity of human beings, and even their relation to the world, should develop in the sporting mode; and the charter should be its written support, its scriptural materialization. In this way the Olympic charter presents itself as humanity's second Bible, locating it in time and space according to a principle just as universal as the Christian Bible's. The essential difference between the two is that in the charter everything is beautiful and pacific, a sort of sporty Paradise on earth. The charter exists to maintain the pure and eternal essence of sport in the face of continuous erosion and damage caused by external contingencies:

war first of all, then politics, violence, doping, racism, xenophobia, fraud, corruption ...

The charter is a way of defending a temporarily pacified civilization – associated with the famous 'Olympic Truce' of Greek antiquity, whose formula however is not featured in the charter itself – thanks to the gathering of the youth of the entire world under its sole banner. But it is not only defensive. It also presents itself as a real blueprint for civilization. The Olympic Charter is not intended merely for its own networks (the national Olympic committees) and the connected sporting world (clubs, federations and so on); it should also be diffused among all the world's peoples. The goal of the Olympic Charter is to 'Olympianize' the planet.

Cities organizing the Games, like London in 2012, commit themselves loudly and clearly to the charter and swear not to depart one iota from its sacred principles. The IOC supervises its scrupulous application. The most frightful dictatorships – fascist, Nazi, Stalinist – vowed fidelity and allegiance to it, as if the sacred text transcended the nature of political regimes, from every form of dictatorship to every form of democracy. Is not the Olympic Charter projected as the expression of the sporting movement itself, free from any taint of politics? In the view of its numerous admirers, the Olympic Charter has remained perfectly immaculate throughout its existence, politically virginal and intact; it aspires to be an apolitical document. One proof of that seems to be the very permanence of the text which, although subjected to repeated and virulent assaults by history, has remained the single and absolute reference of the Olympic and sporting movement, while being modified to adapt to changing realities as perceived by the members of the IOC. But the charter has done more than adapt to society over time; it has adapted society to its own tempo, making the life of societies fall unconsciously into the rhythm of its own timetable: the four-year gap between Olympiads, summer and winter games.

It is not our purpose here to work back to the origins of the text that has become the Bible of the whole sporting movement, or to examine its genesis. Our purpose is to try to understand sport in the context of a globalized capitalist world with its immense tentacular organization and its multiple institutions, of which the IOC and its Olympic Charter are the most powerful instruments. The Olympic Charter cannot be relegated to the domain of law, to the sole question of effective regulation. That would be a superficial view of a text which demands much more thorough analysis, and in particular one able to distinguish between the structure of the text and the Olympic phenomenon itself.

Thus, it would be mistaken at the outset to pay too much attention to the formal aspect of the charter, with its rules, applications, prescriptions, recommendations and injunctions, all in relation to the much more prosaic reality of sport. The disparities and dissonances between the structured text and the physical phenomenon are fully at work even when they are profoundly united at base. The Olympic Charter is quite simply the phenomenal, fetishized form of more complex social realities. It is all presented as if on the one hand there were Olympic law and its expression through the charter, an intangible structure, and on the other the reality of sport as it is, less foggy and ethereal, stripped of ideology, with its baleful entourage of violence, corruption, cheating and doping.

In consequence, the Olympic Charter constitutes a formidable ideological mechanism used not only to conceal but to fabricate lies, mystifications, untruths and illusions whose component elements are woven into the text itself. There may be no better example today, along the lines of those Soviet constitutions of yore – 1936 and the Stalinist 'midnight of the century' – that announced at chapter length the swift arrival of a socialist paradise in one country, and made repeated assertions of their democratic character in a morass of utterly inimitable text. Those constitutions were held by all Stalinists to be the world's most democratic, against a sombre background of flourishing camps and gulags, mass deportations and political murders, especially of Trotskyists, from the late 1920s onward. The Olympic Charter projects an illusion of the same kind: the idea of a moment of fraternity, the iconic dominion of fair play in a more general mission of peace for the duration of the Games, when in reality the usual massacres, terror, crime and torture continue unabated in most of the world's countries, sometimes even in the one hosting the Games (as with China in 2008).

Two hundred and five countries are now adherents of the Olympic Movement and its charter, and tens of thousands of athletes swear allegiance to it and vow to obey it. The athletes' oath runs as follows:

In the name of all competitors, I promise that we shall take part in these Olympic Games, respecting and abiding by the rules that govern them, in the true spirit of sportsmanship, for the glory of sport and the honour of our teams.

The profoundly ideological character of the Olympic Charter cannot therefore be attributed solely to the false consciousness of its supposed adepts, or what is imagined of its broadly ideologized content. Who has read the Olympic Charter from beginning to end? But the fact is that the charter is not only an 'illusion' or 'chimera', but also the expression on the conscious level of the objective appearance it assumes in reality. The Olympic Charter is in some sense the external face of the reality, a text written with great rigour (with its rules, its applications) which performs the function of writ, the great writ of Olympic eternity, the vision of an enchanted world. The ideological character of the charter on the other hand nestles in the heart of the text, as its surface, but both a real surface and a blank one on which the whole phantasmagoria attached to sport can be projected.

That surface, that text if you like, is real enough; but at the same time it masks the charter's internal nucleus or essence, because that can only be perceived through pure contemplation. What can be known of it comes from a reading of surface alone, non-exploratory, non-investigative, throwing no light on the evolution of the charter in historical time, as a moment of history and in its relation to reality as such. So that a merely flat, uncritical reading interprets its complexity as a collection of apparently stable processes. In the social imagination, the charter seems always to have existed, without break or gap. But, of course, quite unlike the way it is imagined, the charter has undergone profound changes linked to global historical processes in the society in which it evolved. The Olympic Charter has had a reciprocal influence on society: during the Olympic festivities, the world is perceived through the prism of the charter.

The fact remains that the charter sets out on paper the 'Olympic Idea' presented as 'the oldest institution of humankind ... one of the last evangelical notions to be accepted by humanity', in the words of a former journalist on the sports paper *L'Équipe*. Comparing the charter with the Bible is thus hardly exaggerated, so great is the devotion to this text, little known and little read, but recited as if it were known by heart, although quite often quoted incorrectly. The charter illustrates the sacred character of the Olympic idea. While the idea is already imbued with a conception of the world with its blocks of seamless myth, harsh ideologies and tenacious prejudices, the Olympic Charter for its part is a successful attempt at codifying political, ideological, moral and cultural positions.

It is worth reading and absorbing the 'Fundamental Principles of Olympism', laid out in six points of a few lines each, for they summarize the Olympic Charter along with its political-ideological foundations. The first principle establishes at the start that Olympism is 'a philosophy of life, exalting and combining in a balanced whole the qualities of body, will and mind. Blending sport with culture and education, Olympism seeks to create a way of life based on the joy of effort, the educational value of good example and respect for universal fundamental ethical principles.' (p. 9). This is already fairly astonishing. How has the principle managed to survive a reality that has battered holes in it for so many years? What could possibly be meant by 'philosophy of life', 'culture', or 'education', when Olympism is known to be stained with repeated misdeeds, crimes, lies, dissimulations, ruses and hypocrisies; with prevarication, peculation and embezzlement even within the Olympic movement's governing body, the IOC itself?

The idea of a 'philosophy of life' is worrying enough for starters. The word 'philosophy' refers to a notion of wisdom, and there is precious little of that in the Olympic Games. Least of all in their mounting inherited excesses, the gigantism to which they endlessly aspire, manifest in colossal budgets and a world-wide scattering of monumental architectural achievements. Baron Pierre de Coubertin may well have wished to establish a continuity with antiquity through the games, but that hardly justifies use of the term 'philosophy' in an essentially rhetorical charter. To use and maintain this term seems almost perverse, when to all appearances it does not apply to any aspect of the Games. In the Greek, *philo* signifies 'love' or 'taste' and *sophos* 'adept', 'prudent' or 'wise'. There was little noticeable wisdom or love about the Beijing Games: titanic organization, mind-boggling budget, urban chaos due to dehumanized edifices erected as propaganda, militarization of sporting venues, permanent police presence inside and outside the stadiums, police supervised by another police, generalized informing, fierce competition between towns to get in on the act, equally ferocious competition between athletes to break records, virtually generalized (but denied) use of performance-enhancing drugs, high-pressure training of 'athletes' (sometimes as young as four or five) in conditions of appalling physical and psychological suffering … the list goes on. So much for the philosophy. There is less of a problem with the word 'life', although the lives of these young people have been taken over, held hostage, forced off course by sport, when they should be enjoying a different sort of youth, spared at least the brutal training and the stupefying effect of endless hours of intense physical exercise.

To that rather specialized philosophy of life, the first principle of Olympism adds the notions of 'culture' and 'education' to 'create a way of life based on the joy of effort, the educational value of good example and respect for universal fundamental ethical principles'. Of these terms, rolled out in the charter with such orotund relish, the easiest idea to accept is 'the joy of effort'. They do seem happy in their way, those sadomasochistic athletes ready to pay with their whole being, prepared to endure extraordinary bodily suffering in pursuit of mad extremes of training. All display an appropriate smile. Athletes are happy in their suffering and suffer for their happiness. In their minds, the bliss of a medal around the neck is doubtless beyond price. The price, the heavy price, will be paid by the body. For 'the joy of effort' in competitive sport leads directly to bodily damage, firstly because of the over-training which athletes endure to high pain levels, and secondly by means, if we may put it this way, of rampant doping.

In such a context 'the joy of effort' carries more than a whiff of meaninglessness, of contradiction in terms. But to get it accepted, and ensure its internalization by future athletes, the simplest way is to impose it on children: systematic rebellion is difficult when you are only four or five. The charter's 'way of life' and 'joy of effort' can look (in China for example) more like party and state violence against the individual – something related to the forms of sporting slavery invented by past and present Stalinist dictatorships (USSR, GDR, North Korea, China, Cuba) and taken up in their essentials by Western democracies, albeit on a smaller scale. But a sporting 'way of life' is a puzzling idea. A way of life is something immense but at the same time covers minutiae, the way people of all sorts act, behave towards each other and relate specifically to the world. A sporting way of life would involve accepting that sport ruled our lives, defined our relation to the world, aspired to educate us all and gave some sort of access to culture.

Real culture, unlike sport, is based on intellectual emancipation, an endlessly renewed flight of the imagination, a relation to the world not focused narrowly on a record or performance to be beaten. Kandinsky and Giacometti did not work to establish a record or wrest a place from another painter or sculptor, even if their works were quickly welcomed by a vast market. Nor is the world projected by art compressed down to the abstract quantification of a jump, a sprint or putting a 16-lb shot; that world is not devastated by the outcome of a match between two teams. And were a sports-based 'way of life' to develop, the result might dismay us. For sport would then no longer be an ancillary activity, but would become a veritable social plan. Sport would no longer be a reflection of society, it would become its prescriptive blueprint on a scale never before attained by any means of mass mobilization, including world religions. But perhaps that is what the charter suggests, and what the charter seeks to promote: not just to make sport an inescapable feature of everyday life, but *to turn everyday life wholly and completely into a sporting activity*.

The second principle of Olympism makes sport responsible for the 'harmonious development of man, with a view to promoting a peaceful society concerned with the preservation of human dignity.' One is again reduced to astonishment: what conceivable harmonious development could come from sport? It has long been the case that certain contests – weightlifting, boxing, the marathon and other long endurance races – involve phenomenal levels of violence and brutal suffering, between and for individuals. Contestants' bodies are not just subjected to severe physical stress, but actually tortured. The sight of weightlifters stuffed with anabolic steroids, mountains of muscle capable of lifting tons of cast iron, arouses no thoughts of 'harmonious development' in a normal observer; nor does 'human dignity' come to mind. The same goes for shot-putters, discus and even hammer throwers of either sex, outlandish monsters of mingled fat and muscle, devoid of the seemliness and proportion that necessarily attend the historical concept of harmony.

So too with sprinters and distance runners, who in the space of a few years have become small robots, greased meteors, packages of dense muscle squirting down the lines painted on the track, racing cyborgs pitted against time and space, a millisecond here, a milli-metre there. Beauty is sometimes mentioned, but there is precious little beauty here, that harmonious proportion of the parts to the whole. To refer back to the Enlightenment, Denis Diderot defined harmony as 'the unity of the whole is born of the subordination of the parts; and of this subordination is born harmony which pre-supposes variety'. Contemporary athletes are far from that sort of harmony when their own physical development so often suggests an imbalance, not to say a rupture of the relation between the parts and the whole under the cumulative effect of gruelling daily training and the prevalence of doping: muscle-bound and hypertrophied or wiry and threadlike, their bodies have adapted to sporting technology and its focus on records.

What has become of beauty? Beauty in its artistic connection is a radical indictment of reality and the often fleeting evoca-tion of a beautiful image. In this context we align ourselves with Kant's endlessly protracted pursuit of a goal, because sport is the exact reverse of the philosopher's theory. Sport has a goal in itself: winning at all costs, beating an adversary or a record at a steep price, through radical transformation of the body, perhaps also by aligning it with irreversible criteria of rationality and standardization. Sport is always shaped by a goal that is utilitarian, inevitable, devouring. Competitive sport is not therefore an indictment of everyday reality, but rather the opposite: a gloomy redoubling of that reality. It is rather an anti-art because, behind the promise of liberation, only its *reification* is attempted. In a later chapter, we will undertake more detailed analyses of the alleged beauty of sport and the implausibility of the sporting aesthetic.

For the moment the question is: Will this metamorphosis of the body be carried out under cover of the IOC and its charter? Will anyone dare to suggest a new harmony, a new beauty, when the sporting body has become an artificial object, a patchwork of grafts? Very thorough experimental studies are being carried out on the ACTN3 gene responsible for fast muscle contraction, PPAR-delta which regulates growth of slow-contracting muscles, the protein IGF-1 (Insulin-like Growth Factor 1) affecting growth, and other genes regulating erythropoietin, a hormone affecting the production of red blood cells. The new wave of Supermen and Wonder Women will soon be wowing us in the stadiums. They will run faster, jump further, throw harder than their shadows. And the charter will still be boasting to us about harmony and beauty.

To all appearances, the extreme specialization of sports in which athletes are trapped leads not to any bodily diversity but on the contrary to standardized, 'manufactured' bodies, the production of bodies machined to the ideal dimensions and configuration for the sport to which they are subjected. Such specialization for competitive sporting practice contributes nothing to the harmonious proportions that, traditionally, appeal to the eye and the intelligence (reason). In competitive sport the gaze, the visual faculty in general, is itself tainted, contaminated, screened as it were by the exclusive focus on the necessary, slanted athlete's gesture and gait, the primacy of the body formatted by and for sporting performance.

Nor can it be said that many demands are made of the intelligence during heats. No sustained reasoning, conceptual logic, careful strategy or even doubt are required to fathom the nature of athletic competition. All the contestants have to do is run, jump, throw and swim ever faster, ever further! Athletes' bodies in consequence are increasingly subjected to a regime of permanent training, of early specialization, of the extreme visualization of bodies deformed by sustained effort in a restricted range.

'The practice of sport is a human right,' the fourth principle of Olympism begins, adding that the Olympic spirit 'requires mutual understanding with a spirit of friendship, solidarity and fair play.' This principle lies at the heart of Olympic ideology. It aspires to place Olympism on the level of the other human rights recognized by sovereign nations. In the case of competitive sport, this is absolute nonsense. Human rights are based on the conviction that every individual, whatever his or her origin, should be protected in terms of civil, political, economic, social, associative and other rights. Individual rights exist in the form of a right to do anything 'that does not harm others'. These include: physical freedom, starting with the right to life, freedom from slavery, torture and inhuman or degrading punishments, freedom from arbitrary detention (habeas corpus); freedom of marriage and kinship (and today the right to privacy); the right to hold private property (enshrined in the 1789 declaration as a natural and imprescriptible human right, articles 2 and 17); contractual freedom (Article 1134 of the French Civil Code). Other human rights are freedom of religion, of conscience, of education, of speech and of association. And of course the political freedoms: to vote, to resist oppression, the right to peaceful assembly, all the labour laws, social support, education, the right to strike, to unionize, and so forth.

How can the Olympic Charter aspire to make the practice of sport a 'right' on a par with the others? There seems to be some confusion over the definition of 'sport'. From the charter's viewpoint, sport is not a normal physical activity like walking, or running then stopping, riding a bike, having a drink, changing direction. When the charter uses the word sport it means competitive sport alone, a codified, institutionalized activity developing its own logic within a world of records, performances, daily training and specialized medicine. It emphatically does not mean sport in the sense of play, a disinterested activity without material goals, ludic and free, but instead an activity that 'requires mutual understanding with a spirit of friendship, solidarity and fair play', in a setting whose 'organisation', 'administration' and 'management' 'must be controlled by independent sports organisations'. Really this expresses the triumph of an extreme and harmful ideology, of words turned upside down. For while a modicum of understanding, friendship, solidarity or even fair play may persist or survive in relaxed, informal, friendly or warm-up activities— football matches or other games with mixed-sex teams and no material outcome—serious competition unleashes behaviour and actions of the worst sort: aggression, violence, bribery, cheating, chauvinist and nationalist attitudes, you name it. In sum, when 'sport' is subject to organization, administration and management controlled by 'independent sports organisations' as specified by the Olympic Charter, one can but fear the worst; and in sport, the worst is the real. The 2008 Beijing Games offered a clear example, being administered, managed and organized not by the City of Beijing (as they should have been according to the Olympic Charter) but directly by the Chinese Communist Party and its Organizing Committee, with the unconditional support of the IOC. After the 2008 Games, can sport reasonably be seen as a disinterested activity, let alone a human right? The Olympic Games seem rather to embody a negation of humanity, a denial of one of its rights, the right established in France by the struggles of 1793: to a life free from all shackles …

The fifth fundamental principle deals with discrimination. 'Any form of discrimination with regard to a country or a person on grounds of race, religion, politics, gender or otherwise [*sic*] is incompatible with belonging to the Olympic Movement.' Not until 1949, to lift remaining 'ambiguities' after the Second World War, did this formulation – present in all subsequent charters – make its appearance. The horse had fled the stable more than a decade earlier with the 1936 Games, used effectively to boost the Nazi regime and its racist, anti-Semitic and xenophobic propaganda.

Berlin 1936, Moscow 1980 and Beijing 2008 were not, then, examples of involuntary skids or avoidable swerves, temporary deviations from the everlastingly straight Olympic road. All three were high points of Olympism, key dates in the history of the Olympic ideal, boosting the images of three different totalitarian regimes – Nazi, Stalinist and bureaucratic-capitalist – by crystallizing them around what sport had already become, with its order, its mafialike institutions, its authoritarian forms of organization; qualities in harmony, one could say, with the enterprise of regimenting people and making them march in step with the aid of a global event and spectacle. The Nazi government, for example, had been quick to grasp that the Games – the 'Nazi Olympiad' – would help with the construction and stabilization of its own state policy by projecting sickening values and justifying evil acts: exaltation of Aryan purity, conversion of Germany into a militarized police state, repression of the main dissidents (communists and Jews) ... The German team's success in winning the most medals was experienced at the time as the Hitler regime's first victory over a world awed by its sporting exploits. Nothing could undermine that, not even the four gold medals won by Jesse Owens, the 'negro' or 'African auxiliary of the US' in Hitler's words. And contrary to what has been widely believed, Owens's victories did not give people pause, or distance them from the bellicose and racist character of Nazi ideology, let alone inspire them to resist it; they raised the existing racial hatred of the hysterical populace in the stands to fever pitch. Each victory unleashed howling waves of Heil Hitlers from an audience rotten to the core, foaming with racist hatred. And in any case, the victories were seen as provocation: how could a subhuman from the distant tribes of Africa, hardly more than an animal, lay claim to a legitimate win against humans?

All accounts show that the Berlin Games were the Games of 'discrimination' against those, fairly numerous one would think, who could not in decency express any allegiance to the regime in place. And sport in Olympic form was to endorse all those forms of discrimination. No country would refuse in the end to take part in the monstrous apotheosis, despite many attempts to organize a boycott. In the final analysis, no confrontation between athletes, no competition would help with any struggle against Nazism; no victory in races, jumps or throws by opponents of Nazism could reverse a now irreversible situation. Before the opening of the 1936 Games no individual, no religion, no country was officially banned. The Nazi bosses themselves, in full agreement with the IOC, forbade any act that might contradict the Olympic Charter's self-styled apoliticism. The logical outcome of the great festival of the whole world's youth would be war, war carried by the Olympic Games as cloud carries a tempest …

Reading through the charter, one soon comes across other glaring contradictions hidden in the text. One is the charter's declared intention 'to lead the fight against doping in sport' (p. 11), when in fact doping is practised on a massive scale in the Olympics despite attempts at surprise detection. The charter aims to 'encourage and support measures protecting the health of athletes', but doping is organized and timed to be at peak effectiveness for the Olympic Games, to say nothing of the truly inhuman intensity of preparatory training. Little concern was shown for the long-term health of the former GDR's female champions, constantly subjected to testing that amounted to torture by doctors and trainers avid for their country's glory. How 'healthy' really is a swimmer who has spent her entire youth doing lengths in a fifty-metre pool? What is the effect on health of lifting cast iron weights for years on end?

There are even more glaring contradictions between the Olympic Charter and Olympic reality. In the section headed 'Olympic Games', the Games are specified as 'competitions between athletes in individual or team events and not between countries.' Nevertheless the flags of participating nations are flown over the stadium throughout the Games; the national anthem of the winner of each competition is played; and the nations are ranked in order of the number of medals won, a classification which can be found on the IOC's website. Finally, although it purports to be transparent about its financial affairs, and despite more than a few scandals over the years, the charter makes it clear that the IOC is far from diffident on these matters:

> The Olympic Games are the exclusive property of the IOC which owns all rights and data relating thereto, in particular, and without limitation, all rights relating to their organisation, exploitation, broadcasting, recording, representation, reproduction, access and dissemination in any form and by any means or mechanism what-soever, whether now existing or developed in the future ...
>
> The Olympic symbol, flag, motto, identifications (including but not limited to 'Olympic Games' and 'Games of the Olympiad'), designations, emblems, flame and torches ... shall be collectively referred to as 'Olympic properties'. All rights to any and all Olympic properties, as well as all rights to the use thereof, belong exclusively to the IOC, including but not limited to the use for any profit-making, commercial or advertising purposes. The IOC may license all or part of its rights on terms and conditions set forth by the IOC Executive Board.

Perhaps that is what is meant by the beauty of sport!

4. COMPETITIVE SPORTS: GLOBALIZED SPORT-SPECTACLE AND NATIONAL FETISH

All through the twentieth century and into the twenty-first, competitive sport has developed against a background of the spectacular and accelerating capitalist globalization now shaking the walls of that narrow but still valid entity, the nation. Sporting competition has spread across all nations, weaving a gigantic moving tapestry of immense power and indestructibility through its visible and invisible economic, political and ideological networks. *Competitive sport is ubiquitous and permanent.* In the cities that organize and mount the events, their streets invaded by races and marathons, by post-match celebrations, by ad hoc sports venues, by stadiums springing up like mushrooms; on posters and advertisements; in special transport arrangements; in the media and mass communications, the press pulsating with sports news, radio, TV and mobile phone coverage, giant public screens in city squares, all united to make sport inescapable, so that everyday conversation is bloated with invasive logorrhoeic blather on the triumph or demolition of some team, the knee injury of some player, the love life of some female champion ... In a word, sport saturates the whole of life with its spellbinding power, so that even the lives of individuals are subjected to sport and its mode of organization. Sporting competition is permanent and universal, with encounters taking place in all cities in all countries in all continents, in all the natural elements: Olympic Games, world championships, World Cup, intercontinental cups, European Cup, national cups; diverse cyclical tournaments and ever more amazing challenges in the air, the sea, the mountains, hog the headlines of the news the world wants to receive. Architects have already planned a stadium on the moon!

Vast territories unhampered by democracy, ultra-centralized governance, celestial bureaucracy, innumerable subjects: competitive sport is today a world power without equivalent. A power in itself alone, with its own institutions on the global, continental, national and local levels (IOC, FIFA, FIA, UEFA, the clubs …), invariably more powerful through those bodies in terms of budget, media presence and ideological clout than institutions like the UN or UNESCO. Sport is globalized by definition through its institutional, supranational structures and tentacular administration, while also sinking its roots into the soil of nations via the various sports federations. Sport is imperialist not only because it colonizes land and destroys people's cultures, but also because of the disappearance of ancient popular practices in favour of a handful of globalized and globalizing sporting disciplines such as football. The sports empire is settling down as a mobile tournament ground, a turntable of exchanges, all organized as a social project adjusted to the world, but breaking down its historical diversity to accommodate a homogenizing globalized sport. You could even say that sport has become the mode or model of the current globalization, not just its reflection but its true blueprint. Its totalitarian character accords with the grip it has over society and individuals, enormously amplified by the media which, contrary to widespread belief, are not its heralds but its followers. *Sport has itself become the world's most powerful mass medium.*

The spectacle of sport, today's sport as spectacle, or more precisely the relation of individuals to sport mediated by images of sport, is the great centrifuge of our time. Sport as spectacle effectively absorbs and kneads to an even consistency a host of facts and images – images that will now pass for facts – to produce a new synthesis and beam it across the world. So that, for example, the idea of nation, when passed through the sporting filter, can quickly become a confused ideological form removed from its original meaning. During a rugby World Cup game in 2007, at a moment when 'France' was doing well, a commentator blurted out: 'The nation is free!' almost as if the rugby team *were* France. When a national team wins a game, the nation itself is celebrated as an institution closely associated with the sport. Celebrations of such euphoria that the true territory of sport might as well be the nation: a restored nation, the legitimate nation, the nation incarnate. Flags are unfurled and waved in the stadium and stuck on house windows, national anthems are sung out of tune by most of the athletes weeping on the podium and the mass of supporters in the stands; national team shirts are worn and national flags displayed above the grandstands (and worn as clothing by some supporters). As if the image of the nation were no longer carried by the people, but by a team; as if the nation's fate were no longer bound up with that of a territory circumscribed by frontiers, but something to be played out in a stadium; as if a common language had been distilled down to the synchronized slogan-bawling of supporters.

So sport as spectacle may help generate a renewal of national unity, much damaged in recent years by the bullying globalization process shaking or displacing the nation-state's references. With nations weakened or even breaking up under the onslaught of glo-balization, sport may seem the last rampart or the last means for individuals to identify themselves, come together and face the inevi-table. Times of war apart, all the great surges of hardcore national feeling now occur over sporting contests. The craze for sport, the dense crowds of like-minded fans, the immediate partisan mass mobilizations, unprecedented in scale, generated by sporting com-petition in city streets and in front of TV screens, illustrate the pitch of chauvinist or nationalist loyalty reached by some individuals in Europe, Africa and Asia.

Sporting nationalism contributes to the unrestrained behaviour of overheated supporters and shares in the generalized violence of which sport is the most visible public manifestation. Everywhere can be found the worship of strength, contempt for weakness, chau-vinism, racism, xenophobia, anti-Semitism, homophobia, verbal and physical violence inside and outside the stadiums, brutality on every ground. Sport is not just the cradle for a resurgence of visceral nationalism but also a new school of violence, and often of racism since the objective is to defeat the adversary, the opposing entity, the Other. This sporting nationalism is unleashed at football matches between national teams. Then, woe betide the vanquished (as they said in ancient Rome), especially when the other is of a slightly dif-ferent skin colour. The argument in France in early 2011 over the issue of quotas (of black and North African players) in the French football team is revealing not just of the discrimination and racism practised by French football managements, but of something people are reluctant to admit: the racism exuded by football itself from every pore. An analysis of the quota idea might arrive at a national sporting prototype: mainly white, not too tall, not too physical, identified with a culture that might be considered French ...

Lastly, in the narrow context of the nation, globalized sporting competition no longer helps to contain violence or to channel it – as academics such as Norbert Elias or Eric Dunning believe – but rather generates and maintains it, spreading it everywhere. In any case, the predominant setting for violence in society is the stadium, along with its immediate surroundings: here, mass emotion is incubated through sound and spectacle, and primitive violence is discharged, especially when rival national teams are playing. Some matches remain memorable for the nationalist passions they unleashed: Chile–Italy in 1962, England–Argentina (1966), Honduras–El Salvador (1969), France–Germany (1982), France–Algeria (2001), Holland–Portugal (2006), Algeria–Egypt (2009), among others. In the space of a few years, the football field has become a miniature battleground for limited confrontation between sporting nations through the agency of their national teams. In the popular imagination, the stadium during sporting contests acquires a particular charge, becoming a formalized setting with a fortified perimeter, its boundaries visible although it is subject to televised globalization which blurs those boundaries out of existence. The historian Eric Hobsbawm has noted:

> Between the wars sport as a mass spectacle was transformed into the unending succession of gladiatorial contests between persons and teams symbolizing state-nations, which is today part of global life. ... International matches actually ... established with the object of integrating the national components of multi-national states ... symbolized the unity of such states, as friendly rivalry among their nations reinforced the sense that all belonged together by the institutionalization of regular contests that provided a safety-valve for group tensions, which were to be harmlessly dissipated in symbolic pseudo-struggles.

In more political terms, we are now (to borrow from and extend the ideas of the sociologist George L. Mosse) witnessing a nationalization of the masses through sport, on a world scale: an internalization and intensification through sport of a nationalism that seemed to have been superseded as a result of globalization. Sport as a spectacle is now a global business, owing to the constant transfer and permanent mobility of players as well as 24-hour TV retransmissions. However, this thoroughly globalized enterprise is constantly checked in its development by the maintenance of the strict national framework in which the sporting institution still sees its true flowering. It is nations that are represented in great institutions like FIFA and UEFA, and even for the Olympic Games in their organizing body the IOC, and the role of nation is fundamental in the living representation of athletes. The award of medals is accompanied by the aforementioned national anthems, and the flags of all nations crown the Olympic stadium …

The central contradiction in sport today, then, stems from the conflictual relations between nation and globalization, between national sportsmen and women and stateless or transnational ones. The legitimacy of the national frame is continuously transgressed, primarily by the existence of international standards – for example the athletics record, which has real meaning as an absolute reference only if it is a world record. National records still exist, of course, but they are hardly significant compared to the universal yardstick of the world record. The *use value* of the national record is metamorphosed into *exchange value* on world terrain. The consequences in the sporting domain are objective and permanent friction between nation and world, between the athlete tied to his nation-state and the athlete projected into the worldwide competition circuit. The resulting chronic crises of the institution have now become structural. The national frame is no longer sufficient for the logic of competition which demands the world as its territory. So the national frame of sport is constantly being battered by the globalizing thrust intrinsic to the internal logic of sport.

5. SPORT:
AS OLD AS THE WORLD?

THE NEW SPORTING ORDER

Obviously, sport is not quite 'as old as the world'. It was born in England, the 'classical' place of origin (according to Marx) of the capitalist mode of production, now planetary in scope. Originally a class practice, sport developed during the nineteenth century in tandem with the consolidation of imperialism. The different sports (rugby, cricket, soccer, athletics) spread to other countries and took root in new territories often colonized through military conquest. Competitive sport owes its rapid development to reduced working hours, the rapid expansion of cities, the establishment of good transport networks and latterly the deployment of an immense media infrastructure. But it makes its own contribution. The sporting institution is a key element of the liberal–capitalist system. Clubs, the basic units of this institution, function effectively as competing enterprises: talented players are bought and sold on to the highest bidder and a sporting proletariat and semi-proletariat, even a lumpenproletariat, have taken shape. The business bourgeoisie was quick to take an interest in the sporting world and rapidly gained control of the clubs and international federations, chasing out hidebound aristocrats and the military.

The sporting institution is consequently integrated into the capitalist mode of production as a specific branch of the division of labour. In parallel with sports 'merchandising' a mass sporting spectacle is created, with its peripheral industries – equipment, regalia – advertising in stadiums for mass-market products, indirect taxes through gambling games. Nevertheless the sporting institution's development lurches from crisis to crisis in its crazed pursuit of exploitation and hegemony over the entire world, all the time. Sporting competition has become permanent and affects every country in the world; anyone with a TV set can follow it day and night, for sports coverage is continuous. But the whole system is regularly rocked by corruption scandals. Embezzlement, bankruptcies and false bankruptcies, match fixing (football, tennis, basketball), frauds of every description, extortion, prevarications leading to constant conflicts of interest, all these are rife.

So sport, in its current socio-political dimension, has little in common with old-world physical contests like real tennis, the many ancient regional variants of football or the polo-like Central Asian game *Buzkashi*, played with a dead goat. It is different by reason of a new *temporality*, both in the practice of sport which is governed by precise chronometric timing and in the ever-accelerating pace of successive sporting events. Space is also invaded and renewed: modern sport has an absolute need to procure spaces; it concentrates itself in strategic spots – stadiums for example – to broadcast the events through television. Nearly all sport takes place in stadium-like circumscribed spaces, inward-looking and with their backs turned to the city. Open-air competitions, running races, bicycle, motorcycle and car races or even ocean races (America's Cup) tend to be held on special tracks – seaways marked by buoys in the latter case – and such facilities are solidly converted or purpose-built, often in concrete, steel and stone. It is only in this type of contained space that sport becomes possible: when it is framed, encircled, surrounded.

What differentiates modern sport from its pre-nineteenth-century precursors is determined by a profound spatial and temporal transformation in an upturned economic setting. The feudal mode of production that reproduced itself in its entirety has been supplanted by the capitalist mode of production, reproducing multinational capital in extended fashion, based on its ceaseless drive to extract surplus value. While the first celebrated an eternal, natural, irreversible order, modern Games legitimize a rational, methodical, efficient social system. The purpose of the Olympic Games in antiquity was a matter of belief in a religious mode, a purpose going beyond the Games themselves, but primarily and essentially Greek; the modern Games are based on an appropriation and dominion of the body as a source of labour power and output. Ancient champions did not seek records, only victory over their rivals. So much for the main differences between ancient and modern sport. But there is also an enduring continuity, a persistence of the ancient in the modern. Seen from a distance the races might look similar, the movements are comparable, the bodily skills not very different. Nevertheless, there is a distinction, a break; there is a hiatus between the two types of sport, although not total because of the continuities and connections that still exist and resist the erosion of time. The roots of modern sport run deep into ancient sport even though everything differentiates them. The fact remains that this widespread difficulty, or sometimes wilful failure, to understand the dialectical relations between ancient and modern is characteristic of an apolitical stance. Karl Marx, in a youthful polemic attacking a political opponent, remarked trenchantly that:

> It is characteristic of … 'sound common sense' … that where it succeeds in seeing differences, it does not see unity, and that where it sees unity, it does not see differences. If it propounds differentiated determinants, they at once become fossilised in its hands, and it can see only the most reprehensible sophistry when these wooden concepts are knocked together so that they take fire.

Beyond this analysis of the permanence of links between ancient and modern sport, it can be said that sport is order because it legitimizes the established order whatever form that may take. Always happy to fit in, never challenging, rarely challenged, sport performs an apologetic function for the dominant mode of production and the system, in which it is not simply a mechanism or geartrain but central to the machine. Sport helps stabilize the current system through mass identification with champions – 'the gods of the stadium' – and the resulting depoliticization, by rationalizing massive myths (such as that of healthy competition between individuals), constantly stressing the natural hierarchy of strength and weakness, reproducing social inequalities under cover of a pseudo-equality between participants, constituting what amounts to a compact socio-ideological and practical lobby, and setting up what can only be called a production line of selection, training, competition, performance, records, etc. Sport has become the new opium of the people, more alienating than religion because it suggests the scintillating dream of a promotion for the individual, holds out the prospect of a parallel hierarchy. The element of 'protest' against daily reality that even religion (according to Marx) still retained is stifled by the infinite corrosive power of sport, draining mass consciousness of all liberating and emancipatory energy.

Competitive sport seizes hold of the body and prepares it for work as 'free' labour power to be exploited or displayed. The principle of corporeal output and productivity of the organism is the self-evident principle of sport, hence the mechanization and Taylorization of movements and the vaunted morality of effort, against a background of ideological and political neutrality. The mode of domination characterizing athletes' relation to their bodies is basically sadomasochistic, inflicting suffering and rejoicing in suffering. Sport could lay claim to being a powerful instrument of de-eroticization of the sensory and muscular apparatus.

All authoritarian regimes have made use of sport to regiment their youth by encouraging authoritarian, aggressive personality structures, and most of all to ensure blindly obedient masses. In the stadiums built for the Olympics and for the various world and regional championships and cups (athletics, football, rugby), the spectators become enormous concerted crowds, separate individuals coming together and blending into an aggregate that itself offers a mass spectacle, broadcast across the world by television. Inside the stadiums, the involvement in the sporting spectacle of these 'masses in a ring' (Elias Canetti), welded into an effective visual and sound instrument, is total, with a conviction passed on to the infinitely larger TV audience. *The order of the mass is a mass of order.* Inside these places, the mass discharges its aggressive impulses in an – often frightening – catharsis mechanism. The totalitarian compacting of the individuals bringing the stadium to life by becoming part of it is an important factor in the *emotional fascization* of great crowds in the visual and aural grip of an accepted and expected order: solemn processions, award ceremonies, national anthems, salutes to the flag, not to mention the violent and murderous clashes between athletes in the more popular competitions. The imposition of internal order inside the stadium with its barriers, stewards and CCTV surveillance is completed by the order often imposed during important encounters by military and police all over the city and outside and inside the stadium. The stadium's sporting order endorses and reflects a politics of order.

6. ORIGIN AND DEVELOPMENT OF THE *THESES* ON THE CRITIQUE OF SPORT

PROGRESSIVE GLOBALIZATION THROUGH SPORT

The 'Theses on the Critique of Sport' (see Appendix I) – advanced in the post-May '68 period – have lost none of their intrinsic theoretical force, even if their following in the academic (school and university) sectors originally associated with them has fallen away during the intervening decades. Nor have those theses lost their prophetic character, though here too reality has followed fiction and even overtaken it. When the theses were written by a small group of intellectuals eager to come to grips with a steel-hoofed Moloch, they resounded like a thunderclap in a political sky already far from serene, with social mobilizations, strikes and struggles on a scale not seen since the brief heyday of the Popular Front in the 1930s. We were still inside the May '68 shockwave. We've come a long way since then …

These writings marked an advance in the critical theory of sport by throwing light on a hitherto unidentified and unthinkable phenomenon: a blind spot in the centre of what was then seen primarily as a simple social practice, individual or collective, a moment of happiness, a relaxation, a leisure activity, a form of play. In short a social phenomenon regarded – obviously wrongly – as independent of politics, a feature of mass leisure, linked to the yearning for entertainment then surfacing in the new urban petty bourgeoisie as it sought to imitate its inaccessible big sister. The main debates on sport in that distant time concerned its political character, the quarrel opposing amateurs and professionals, its effects on health … In those days, one was not supposed to associate what was considered part of normality, amusement, leisure, social phenomena of great 'purity', with politics which is a lot less pure, what with its bickering, controversies, arguments, latent or open confrontations between diverse opinions, dirty tricks and often sordid reality. Remember that in the early 1970s – and for a long time afterwards – sport was still regarded as being above the social and political scrum, and invariably beneficial to those practising it or even just watching it.

At that already remote time, the very idea of objecting to the increasingly globalized reality of sport, or suggesting a critical understanding of it, seemed outrageous to many, for sport was a social phenomenon that did not permit reflection, let alone thought, and aroused absolutely no opposition. For although in the post-May '68 period most of the main institutions (school, army, family, art, justice) had been subjected to uncompromising criticism, sport seemed to have escaped opprobrium and was regarded as above suspicion, despite the participation of a few sportsmen in, for example, the occupation of the French Football Federation (FFF) headquarters. Sport had still not been subjected to the same radical interrogation as most of the other institutions thought to be imprisoning and stifling French social and political life. But although anti-sporting critical theory, from which the 'Twenty theses on sport' had emerged, had not been incorporated into the general movement of dissident ideas but remained relatively isolated in the journal *Quel corps?*, it had at least started to analyse what had really penetrated the consciousness of the masses to mobilize them with such evident effectiveness.

It is worth recalling the huge popular fervour in France that followed the French victory in the 1998 football World Cup, marking a sort of consecration of sport as a mass phenomenon able to release an immense amount of energy amplified by the unified mass. The same phenomenon of the growing power of mass sporting mobilization was apparent in 2006 during the German World Cup, once the French team qualified for the final stages, then for the final itself watched in France by a television audience of twenty-five million. Once again the entire country saw a convergence of masses thirsting for victory, establishing what Max Weber might have called a sporting 'emotional community'. The sporting shockwave of the 2007 Rugby World Cup followed a similar course – despite diabolical organization, permanent televisual overkill and the press kowtowing to the new gods of rugby – until it was stopped dead by the French XV's defeat. Sport visualizes itself only in victorious mode.

It can be said that the ideas in the journal *Quel corps?* (1975) embodied the concepts of the critique of sport at the time. In Hegelian terms, they made it possible to expose the sporting *zeitgeist* which has now changed so greatly from that period when a critical spirit still flourished. The theses made it possible to assess, during major globalized competitions, the phenomenal, unprecedented mobilization through sport of immense numbers of individuals on a world scale. In the space of a few years, sport became exactly what *Quel corps?* had predicted: the greatest worldwide mass phenomenon of the twentieth century, and doubtless the new, true religion of the twenty-first. On the other hand, the journal had failed to under-stand the full implications from the viewpoint of possible opposition, because it underestimated the power of sport to imbue society to its depths, its lightning propagation and the mechanisms of its con-tamination. For sport always draws its main strength from worldwide acceptance, acceptance by everyone; sport engages immense masses crammed into the stadium or gathered in front of TV screens (at home, in the pub or bar or in front of a big public screen), masses that pour out afterwards and disperse through the streets to celebrate *their* victory.

By virtue of its local, national and international structures, sport has risen to the level of a *world power*, an authority that tends to obscure, overhang and infuse all activities in a society ravaged by the disarray of mutilated individuals, without any collective project. Sport has established itself as the spearhead of an army in battle order, which crushes anyone who is stupefied by it. The steamroller of decadent modernity, sport flattens everything as it passes and *becomes the sole project of a society without projects.* The world is being coloured by sport. It is the present world medium that unifies all individuals from all religions, social classes and ideologies. As a world power, sport is not only a solidary, uniting, unifying force but the very mode and model of the current globalization. And if sport is globalized, it also 'globalizes', in the sense that it projects globally the smallest events connected to it. A trivial piece of sports gossip can be hoisted onto the global level; and what is global today, for many people, has to do with sport.

What was until a few years ago still of the ordinary mass order, an ephemeral gathering for events circumscribed in a short lapse of historical time, has more recently acquired from globalization a new quantitative surge and what can only be called a qualitative leap. For sport is no longer just an ephemeral but spectacular moment, a time circumscribed by the event, like the World Cup or the Olympics. In football, for example, the spectating mass dressed in Nike or Adidas shirts, the colour-daubed strip of its favoured team, bawling songs of hate against the hereditary enemy, is now drawn out into a sort of sporting global village, a worldwide community in thrall to sporting spectacles and events. The coagulated mass during the sporting event, compressed in its space-time by television broadcasting, is now dilated into a new sporting time which has itself become everyday time. In recent years we have witnessed the emergence of a world sport-mass with its sacred spaces (stadiums), its unique time-frame with games retransmitted day and night (television), its action (permanent competition). So the spectacle of sport is totalitarian in the sense that it achieves the difficult task of uniting time, space and action with a *superior unity* between a time, a space and an action mediated by sport.

In the mid-1970s, the 'Vingt thèses sur le sport' (Twenty Theses on Sport) that emerged from analyses in the journal *Quel corps?* were seen as exaggerated, inappropriate and even dangerous, especially by the Stalinists of the French Communist Party. Most of the ideas were, however, in tune with what was already under way: the establishment of capitalist planetary sport as a complete system with fast-growing autonomy; the emplacement of national, European and international institutions (FFF, UEFA, IOC, FIFA, FIA, etc.); the development of sport as a specific branch of the division of labour with its vast market (rapid expansion of equipment manufacturers of every sort and of a specific athletes' market; sale, transfer or loan of players); the deployment of sporting spectacle through the proliferation of stadiums and retransmission of games through home TV sets and giant video screens inside stadiums and in city squares (and today by a number of channels devoted exclusively to sport); the multiplication of financial scandals and the drift towards racketeering; the generalized doping in all sporting disciplines. All such phenomena were still in their infancy by today's standards.

The 'Twenty Theses on Sport' struck a sharp blow against the sport-sodden society they had been written to oppose and whose true face they exposed. Apart from that, the ideological functions of sport have never been more effective than they became in the 1970s, especially with respect to the legitimization of the established order (winning at all costs, performance, money first); the cultivation of an indiscriminate positivism (total competition, the reign of 'even more', dazzling health thanks to sport); the regimentation of youth (incorporated as an amorphous, depoliticized mass); the sexual repression specific to athletes (love either bracketed between competitions or instead promoted as a warm-up for same); the engineering of what Adorno called the 'desexualization of sex'; the growing use of drugs which tends to eliminate all sex drive with the added prospect, not to put too fine a point on it, of early death – athletes are starting to accept this as inevitable ... All these functions have continued to evolve, grow and take further strides in their organization and structure.

7. THE STADIUM: CONSOLIDATION OF THE MASSES

This chapter deals with the efficacy or effectiveness of the stadium, the most favoured setting for sporting competition. Without a venue for sport, there is no sport. The stadium is that venue, its architecture tailored to permit the fullest organization and diffusion of sporting competition.

To go straight to the point, we note that the stadium is primarily the ideal setting for sporting spectacle, a spatial form devoted almost exclusively to sport for the masses. With the stadium as intermediary, the energies and motivations – social, political, ideological – of thousands of individuals are reorganized, then exploited and amplified according to the internal logic of the sporting spectacle being enacted in the stadium. The stadium channels, unifies and crystallizes an amalgam of individual comportments and collective agitation in a process of *mass repressive social sublimation and desublimation*, channelling energies and impulses associated with political motivations and reorganizing them with a view to their discharge. There are seven principal consequences:

- In the stadium during competitions, there occurs a cyberneticization of the sensory receptors (eye, ear), a general reorganization of the apparatus and processing of the senses of hearing and sight. Sight is the main sense employed to construct the spectacle, with the stadium itself as the frame and the pitch as the sole focus of interest, along with the stands opposite and/or the giant video screen … a deeply impoverished visual field;

- The entire individual is absorbed in the sporting spectacle by transformation of the free enjoyment of the senses into their alienation, through a denial of the individual body to the profit of a unified bodily bloc – the spectator mass – which is desensualized and de-eroticized; a stadium-body is mobilized, a vast coercive battery of serially wired bodies. Inside the stadium, goals by the home team are greeted with howls of unrestrained joy; gloomy silence follows defeat; people are instinctively animated by hatred of the other, the adversary;

- The mass application of an elementary characterology of the individual identified with a visual and sound system wholly inaccessible to the intellect. The violence of seeing is constantly activated by the violence of successive shocks arousing extraordinary emotions; seeing means literally accepting violence and internalizing it as one's vector of inclination; seeing also means being in permanent shock without being aware of it;

- The absence of all criticism, or rather the impossibility of the critical component in connection with a sporting spectacle whose only object is victory at all costs;

- Since the 1980s a sort of 'sporting war' has developed, with its triumphs, accidents, crimes and dramas (Heysel, Hillsborough); this death pandemic is in the process of spreading to all grounds, becoming an irreversible component of sport;

- The abandonment of methodical questioning of what is seen, in favour of an 'affirmative culture': that which is offered to our eyes and ears is beautiful or intellectually satisfying: the technical move, the faulty decision;

- The general absence of critical reflection or self-awareness, leading to the impossibility of a sustained conversation above the level of pub chat and banter.

The stadium implies a radical and unilateral investment in seeing, in the visible, and in everything in the visual order. The sense of 'seeing' is suspended from the sporting spectacle, which in return constructs it into the major organ associated with sporting violence. Seeing no longer means perceiving, distinguishing, glimpsing, let alone reflecting, doubting etc. Seeing in a stadium means accepting what is in front of you as irrevocable, unalterable, incorruptible, positive, obvious, open. This helps explain the ease with which doped athletes are accepted. If they are there, to perform movements in the stadium, 'freely', their mere presence in the holy precinct designates them as untouchable. Indeed, they have now become so. For being an athlete now means being drugged up to the eyeballs with the general consent of the powers that be (sporting community, institutions, state, etc.), or even in response to a pressing social demand: the more doped the sportsmen are, the better their performances, and the more 'sublime' the spectacle in the stadium. A spectacle does not have to be exclusively sporting, but a spectacle ought – according to the report by the 'Grands Stades Euro 2016' commission – to be appropriate to the stadium (the football Euro 2016 is to take place in France). Among that report's many strong recommendations is that stadiums should be 'models of comfort and security. External access facilities (road links, public transport, parking), internal comfort (heated corridors, escalators, electronic ticketing), optimal security and viewing arrangements (CCTV surveillance, reception and working facilities for press and media) combine to *make the stadium not only the setting for the spectacle, but an actual element of it*' (my emphasis).

What is a stadium? And why is it the scene of global violence, both physical (street brawls, scuffles in the stands and blows, foul tackles and brutal acts on the field) and verbal (racist and xenophobic catcalls, destructive cries from the stands when supporters want their teams to 'destroy' or 'smash' the opposition, to 'get stuck in'…)? What makes the stadium the very source and nursery of this 'emotional plague', which we have illustrated with reference to football but which could be extended to cover sport in general?

Firstly, a stadium is a perimeter raised against the outside, a structure with its back turned to the city. It presents itself as a zone uncontaminated by the city (even though most stadiums are within cities), a clean place, cleared of all ideology associated with the chaotic urban world, and where all who enter set aside their normal relation to the world. The athletes involved – physically in their case – are reduced to what their bodies are. Transformed by the iron law of the record book, athletes are the new monsters of the stadium, doped-up gods, absorbing massive doses of powerful but undetectable body- and performance-enhancing products, doing the thing to which they are totally dedicated. In that clean enclosure, uncontaminated by the urban chaos from which it is segregated, athletes can only appear all the more healthy. And paradoxically, watching athletes perform on the track or field makes them seem above suspicion: for a start they are handsome specimens, without any ties, sovereign in their movements and demeanour, superior, invulnerable in their presence. Nor is the doping that nowadays underlies performance and records perceived as cheating or a 'bane'; on the contrary, it is equally seen as a consecration of the champion. The stadium that encloses athletes and spectators is a structure of 'hypervisualization' that amplifies the crowd's frenzies and stimulates the athletes in the psychic frame of a *gigantic collective narcissism*: the fused mass draws a concerted breath only in order to howl in unison, like a bunch of small babies left in the same room for a while.

A spatial crucible in which the gaze is drawn by the body language of sporting competition (or, appreciation of the intense rationalization of the competing body under the primacy of specific and architecturally adapted 'techniques of the body', in Marcel Mauss's phrase) releases at a stroke all the sublimated energies of the mass. The mass completes the living circuit specific to the place, and its surface (the spectators in the stands) becomes an outer 'skin' twitching and rippling with the whole range of emotions, blotched too with eruptions of neurosis. As with the visual, so with the aural: during a game, the energies of increasingly hypnotized spectators are released in surges of sound, a mass wave-form surface like a thick sticky liquid, rising and falling in volume with the emotional state of the mass. The spectating mass in the stadium 'builds' itself into a profoundly unified 'architected' surface, in total symbiosis with the concrete and steel frame whose vibrant and rippling skin it has become, with a liquid, slick sound-surface animated by a living emotional wave. In the geometrical perfection of the stadium, communicated and amplified by the surging mass of the crowd, a range of impulses is 'released': aggression, hatred, murderous sadism, underlining the effect of bringing individuals together while subjecting them to a brutal desublimation of their senses. In this way, the process at work in sporting spectacle takes on its full power in the stadium. It is a regressive phenomenon leading to a degradation of individual awareness and the disintegration of the individual ego in favour of a spatially dominant superego (itself the articulation of abstract, reified visual and aural dimensions).

This desublimation of the senses works most directly on the

hearing, the sense most intimately connected to the individual. The stadium is a mass of fused sound, the blank aural unity of a crowd voluntarily deaf to itself. The spectating mass, put acoustically into a trance state by its chants, shouts, eructations and so on, 'spatializes' itself by deploying its own surface and its own volume, in relation to the *authoritarian architectural design* of the structure – a monumental ring. The stadium is something like a spatialized transposition of the mass voice. For the acoustic spatiality specific to the stadium is at the junction of the technical possibilities offered by the setting with the mass in place: resonance, echo, vibration, the spasm of the compacted mass, can be extremely intense. The quality of the stadium's space is associated with its capacity for resonance. When the spectators react for or against one team or the other, as the tension rises and the crowd starts to roar, that is the moment when the stadium takes on its true dimension. In other words, the spatial quality of a stadium is not so much determined by its shape – round, oval or rectangular – as by its capacity to hold, contain and return the voice of the mass.

The intensity of that voice ranges from simple scattered shouts to the bellowing hysteria of a crowd invaded by the power of its own voice, almost in a trance. Usually, the voice of the mass tries to be tuneful when chanting partisan songs, often warlike in tone, in support of its team. All supporters have their own songs, a way of taking possession of the stadium with the voice. At a stroke, the stadium reconfigures or re-spatializes itself in the grip of that sonorous power. Its impact on the mass is enormous; the voice reverts to the mass, recomposing it as a homogeneous bloc. The voice of the mass enables the mass to be a voice. The voice of the mass gradually becomes one voice, and it fabricates or configures a unique space subject to that voice alone. In this way, the stadium becomes an immense block of sound, the spatial unity of the voice itself able to 'challenge' the space of the stadium. The voice of the mass, like an event horizon in space/time, is capable of modifying the place when at maximum intensity. It can alter perception of the lines, the surfaces, even the volume of the stadium.

The space is not dissolved by the mass voice; more exactly, it undergoes a sort of dematerialization. The voice springs from the depths of each individual spectator and combines with other voices to constitute a de-singularized mass of sound; each individual voice is buried in the mass voice. But voices are the living heart of the stadium. The voice has powerful effects on the nature of the space in the stadium. We mentioned a transformation of the space experienced by the spectators. What is the nature of this transformation? We need here to think in terms of a sort of degradation or decay of space. This does not mean a loss or alteration or deficit of space. The stadium's spatiality, the internal space, becomes all the more present and pregnant. Under pressure of the mass voice and because of its built frame, the stadium suffers a kind of amputation of its depth dimension. The space in the stadium has no perspective; it is pure finite geometry, with no depth of visual field, no infinity to rest the gaze. In a word, it is a *dark space*, empty of values. Remember that the mass forms a ring; it is closed off from the outside as it is from itself. The spectator mass sits facing itself. Thus the visible character of the mass is both amplified and veiled by the mass voice. The simple geometric shape of the ring is sound first and foremost, but against a visual background: *seeing yourself without looking at yourself*. When the mass sings, chants, vibrates, when it asserts its own rhythm by bawling deafening slogans, stamping its feet or performing ill-coordinated 'waves', it is only accentuating its character as a pure agitated surface. This degradation of the space is connected to a valorization of time, but an abstract time, the time of the competition through which the mass voice is constructed in the stadium and, more exactly again, is spatialized. The acoustic universe of the stadium tends in a paradoxical way to promote a generalized autism. Not one with every spectator closed into a bubble hermetically sealed around him; the bubble is bigger, more collective, it is the stadium itself in which every spectator, every insular individual is organically linked to his neighbour, by osmosis as it were. However, the important, the decisive thing is not to see his neighbour next to him or opposite, but to participate together in that vast sonorous background in which every individual can hold his impoverished existence to be valid and even essential.

Inside the stadium, the mass voice shares in the general aggressiveness. It is used to invade the stadium, to conquer it with the power of an immaterial fluid rising from the depths of the spectating and supporting mass. A sonorous line takes shape, a resonance that has no equivalent, the loud diffuse sigh of a powerful volume of sound being projected into space. It is that acoustic volume that displaces the space in the stadium, that is substituted for it. Just as the individual voice comes from the whole body, the mass voice comes from the body of the mass, from the mass as a body. So experiencing the mass voice is not the same as experiencing the voice as a constituent of the body's space. Nor is it even the experience of a dialectic between inside and outside; while the single voice recentres the body, and thus still embodies that dialectic, in the stadium experience the voice of the mass engulfs the individual voice in a booming, totalitarian – because depersonalized – sonority, in the unique temporality made possible by the stadium (chants, melody, screeching, etc.) The mass voice creates its own sound space and its own time. But the mass voice can drive people towards delirium or mass hysteria, and stoke the unease of a mass bloated by its own voice. The individual voice is dispossessed of all its qualities, timbre, tone, texture … As a form of spatial projection from the body diffused into its surroundings, irradiating with sound all the space within range, the individual voice emerges from an inside into an outside. But, in the stadium, the voice of the mass is all external; an effusion of the bodily mass that projects an envelope whose contours are those of the stadium, its terraces, its spectators. If normally the voice is released out of the body towards the Other, in the stadium on the contrary the mass voice is an intrusion into the other, an accepted violence towards Others. It is the appropriation by the internal surface of the stadium, and by its canopy, of the mass voice reconstituted as a single voice.

If the stadium space predisposes to a form of aggressiveness, the mass voice multiplies its effects tenfold. The aggressiveness of the single mass voice causes a distortion of space, a compression rather than an expansion, certainly a radical loss of perspective in the sense that all horizons have vanished, in what is an almost sadistic annihilation of space. The mass voice in the stadium is magical because it is invisible, all-enveloping and immediately seductive. The ring shape of the stadium concentrates and amplifies the mass voice, to define the stadium as an anti-perspective, a space without a horizon, that distant line that stays forever out of reach. The gaze of each spectator is rendered blind by this economy of the face-to-face, of the mirror image, of plain identity. The space is closed off by the looping line of the stands on which the 'stagnant mass' as Elias Canetti calls it – and we would add, vociferous too – has imprinted itself.

To return to what we were saying: perspective being the dialectical aspect of the experience of space, a spatial dimension that is partially temporalized, it follows that the stadium also tends to degrade awareness because the mass voice is generated within an artificial temporalization. Individual awareness, as a structure of anticipation and a capacity for judgement and critical perception, is totally annihilated in the stadium. The phenomena of ecstasy and delirium generated and amplified by the stadium are not anodyne. Thus, following some exploit on the field, a roar arises 'spontaneously' from the mass. It is these roars, whatever their cause, that express the mass and give it its psychic space, but they also demolish any conscious, aware focus on the world. Sometimes, the kind of trance that can arise in a stadium is an effect of the 'constant repetition of the same refrains'. In Philippe de Félice's view, 'all who have some experience of public gatherings know that there is no better or quicker way to bring those present to a state of veritable automatism. A short sequence of syllables, if possible devoid of exact meaning, recurring repeatedly in a very simple and strongly rhythmic musical phrase, soon induces a sort of trance state.'

Sound, in the stadium associated in a particular way with the visual, is deployed there like a thick, invisible mass. Its apparently 'free' or 'spontaneous' deployment should not be misunderstood: the process stems from an initial 'aggressive impulse' which is driven and pumped up by the deep and irresistible sound-swell, shaping individuals in their flesh, assailing them ceaselessly throughout the game, running through their bodies and eliminating all possibility of conscious, aware scrutiny of the sporting event itself or the behaviour it triggers. Gripped by the acoustic aggressive impulse impregnating the mass, the individual ego is as though carried away by or buried under the mass; and the mass is by now in a semi-anorganic state, weighted down, 'releasing' nothing but hatred and sadism in the physico-acoustic order against the Other. In other words, the bodily ego is modelled in the stadium by the spectating community's sound mass. The ego assimilates this vibrant mass through the intermediary of a sound component: the individual's sole object of interest or identification is the bellowing mass of which he is part, a congealed mass immersed in a sometimes overheated tub. Let us recall the nickname for Saint-Étienne's home stadium, 'le Chaudron' – the cauldron which the stadium represents, and the 'symbol of a mass that is no longer disintegrating', as Elias Canetti puts it.

The stadium really is a place of sound incubation, a sound-collector, the setting for an acoustic spell that suggests the possibility of an orgasmic fusion between the individuals and the architecture surrounding them, but also a fusion with the same architecture as something that structures everything they do while they are there. The stadium engenders the possibility of an extreme confusion between collective orgasm and the morbid conduct that stems from the individual's feeling of dissolving, losing, melting his conscious self inside a macrocosm.

8. SPORT, CULTURE AND YOUTH

The rapid and efficient rise of sport is linked to the easy enrolment of the young. They are the social base for the rapid deployment of competition. Their regimentation has nothing to do with the fact that competitive sport may be imposed by the formative institutions they pass through, whether school, family, club or firm, nor with the hypnotic power of omnipresent, inescapable television. This regimentation is something like a vast consensual movement into which a large part of the youth has thrown itself with a spirit and faith only rarely seen before, and on very different terrains: in struggles against military service, educational 'reforms', the extreme right ... In other words, where it had to be coerced in the past, the youth has rallied massively to the new sporting enterprise of its own free will, appointing itself the bard of a 'soft dictatorship' of which it has been the object and, even better, the active subject.

It is worth a short digression here to reflect on the complete reversal of the political position of the young in the advanced capitalist countries and France in particular since the 1980s, when they were constantly instrumentalized by movements like the anti-racist movement SOS-Racisme – 'adult' political groups – and ended by turning back in on themselves. The present goals of the young, their wishes, their life plans, are developing in a conformist register, in an environment of consent to the mainstream values of society, and much less in a critical spirit towards it. While the young are often content to appear like each other, this is mostly a matter of getting ahead of others in a more or less explicit form of competition, in the playground or the leisure park, for example – confected for them by adult class society. From being a force of radical opposition to society, the youth has more or less capitulated to forms of mass-market navel-gazing; it has split off into Gay Pride marches and other macro-enterprises, or brain-rotting new technologies (iPods, MP3s, smartphones etc.); it has become depoliticized to the point of apathy or surrender to the innumerable screens foisted on it, to which it glues itself without a thought for critical distance. Its own idols and icons, credible-seeming public figures such as Yannick Noah, Zinedine Zidane and David Beckham, are often involved in providing sporting spectacle and sport has thus become youth's natural décor and backdrop.

Does today's youth still embody that once-powerful force of anti-capitalist struggle with its institutional 'targets' of family, school and military service? Although the young may manifest discontent over such proposals as the 'contrat première embauche' (first job contract), and a small number of them may rise up against 'business–university' (the law on 'freedoms and responsibilities of universities'), the majority are integrated into society as a pre-proletarian layer vulnerable to appalling working conditions, often unemployed, clinging to brain-deadening gadgets and rejecting any utopia that does not seem expedient or directly bankable. That depoliticizing process is presently being 'materialized', in a sense, through the 'sportification' of young minds. Some may remember from 1998, not without alarm, the enormous, mainly youthful crowds who, abandoning the TV screens to which they had been glued for days, faces flabbergasted by the result – 'Victory is in us!' – poured into the streets of French cities to celebrate the French victory in the World Cup final, flying the French flag, wearing the tricolour shirts of their champions, baying at the tops of their voices outside the presidency of the French Republic for a sight of Zidane and chanting his name ad nauseam in front of his giant portrait projected on the Arc de Triomphe.

It was from that moment that the youth – supported by intellectuals de-intellectualized by sports fever, like Alain Finkielkraut and Edgar Morin, and by eminent journalists, including the editor of *Le Monde*, hypnotized by the beauty of the stadiums and their living gods – exposed itself without any reserve to a form of self-dispossession. Through love of football (followed by rugby) and its idols, the happy excitement of togetherness at the heart of the sporting event, the perfect well-being brought about by reacting in unison this way and that during some final, sport had found its most passionate devotees among the youth, its biggest audience and perhaps its ideal mass. Might not French youth (and something similar would also apply to other youth across the world) have found or recovered in that victory (by *les Bleus*, a team of young men accompanied by wives and girlfriends), as in most of the 'victories' granted or attributed to the young (in the TV game shows whose winners are usually young, in the front- and gossip-page coverage of teenage actors and pop stars, young millionaires and so on), something that in recent years had been objectively lacking: a permitted and acknowledged place, a standing, a role and function, albeit under supervision and as it were by proxy? In a rapid double movement (worthy, one might think, of the football field) the young have projected themselves into the sporting spectacle, of which they constitute the main live audience and the vast majority of practitioners. The 'appropriation' of sport is expressed in a uniform wardrobe of trainers or sneakers, tracksuit bottoms and tee-shirts. Sharing a language steeped in sports references, gulping energy drinks and special food supplements, the young are now imprisoned in a sporting lifestyle.

How can we recognize the current sports craze, fed by the popular identification with athletes, football and rugby stars in particular, without recognizing the key role of sport in severing the young from their former role as a 'natural' opposition force? For it is of course in entertainment, in gadgets and now in sport that the young as such have found themselves in recent years, changing profoundly in the process. A whole 'culture' of which sport was the spearhead, not to say the main vector, has quietly taken shape within the respective youth populations of urban countries (but also in the less developed countries of Africa and Latin America). The change is particularly noticeable in France and Italy, whose youth had for many years been passionately engaged in political campaigning. That is where the political-ideological volte-face seems especially abrupt. So the young have donned the clothes of sport to connect with mass diversion; they have absorbed the sporting universe through an omnipresent television that associates (one should note), in a well-managed confusion, competitive sport with entertainment, enjoyment and something more pernicious: the generalized mockery of everyone and everything in idiotic and perverse reality shows.

What does this tell us about today's society and culture? 'The common culture of any late twentieth-century urbanized culture,' Hobsbawm reminds us, 'was based on the mass entertainment industry – cinema, radio, television, pop music – in which the elite shared, certainly from the triumph of rock music onwards, and to which intellectuals no doubt gave a highbrow twist to make it suitable for elite taste … as when a Puccini aria sung by Pavarotti found itself associated with the World Football Cup in 1990'. Adorno and Horkheimer thought that 'To be pleased means to say Yes. … Pleasure always means not to think about anything, to forget suffering even where it is shown. Basically it is helplessness. It is flight; not, as is asserted, flight from a wretched reality, but from the last remaining thought of resistance. The liberation which amusement promises is freedom from thought and from negation.' The picture is clear enough and the view quite dismissive. Sport has become a mass 'entertainer', the model for generalized competition and, finally, the black hole which has swallowed – without any sign of critical reserve on their part – the young, along with most intellectuals and a good few journalists.

The present development of sport is characterized by the unification and homogenization of the spectator crowds now definable as masses all over the planet. The real challenge of such a profusion of sport is not to catalogue the 'cretinization' of those masses, already quite advanced, but to measure the success with which the masses, especially the young, are being integrated into the sporting spectacle of which they have become protagonists, second only to the athletes themselves.

9. THE SPORTING CHAMPION: ADDICTION AND DRUGS

The birth in the late nineteenth century of modern competitive sport under the guidance of Pierre de Coubertin, and the start of its extension across the planet thanks to a capitalism in full expansion – the new material power liberating the old economy from slavery and other backward, inefficient historical vestiges – brought forth a new type of human being known as the sporting champion. Like the worker emancipated from certain historical restraints (serfdom or slavery) who sells his labour power to the highest bidder (in that sense the worker is 'free'), the athlete has been able to deploy his labour power with equal freedom all over the planet. Today, however, a new historical phase seems to be taking shape following the neo-liberal stabilization of the capitalist system in the richest countries, and its extension into less controlled lands (China, India …), so that capitalism is now broadly accepted as the ultimate and impassable horizon of human social evolution.

The sporting champion being recognized as a social model is not only the traditional, immortal champion, the object of great idolatry that we know. Certainly, the champion carries the idea of efficient physical dexterity and a technique worthy of emulation. The champion represents the active body, now one of the arts of living. Marcel Mauss in his day shrewdly observed the way bodily techniques were transmitted during children's education, and ana-lysed training through submission of the body. Today those bodily techniques are started up by sport, with the wide collaboration of the mass media. But the principal mediator of this social image of the body is the champion, the sporting hero. Identification with champions works through widespread identification with images of the sport-sculpted – 'sportified' – body. The champion is projected as a model surpassing the common, wretched, earthly corporeal condition. He or she is invested with the wish for omnipotence that characterizes magical thought; their body is above average, it exceeds the norms. And its social function has been further enlarged since it became the main vector of the immense mediatization focused on it. The gaze of society has centred on the image of the champion, while at the same time that image has itself been transformed. For the athlete's body, colonized by the enormous technology of medical science, no longer really belongs to him. It is more than apparent that the irresistible advance and definitive interference of doping in sport have modified the champion's body, its image, and the gaze brought to bear on it.

The present status of doping – unanimously condemned outside the sporting institution (by politicians and journalists) and unanimously accepted, sometimes encouraged, inside it (by trainers, doctors and managers) – has led to the emergence of a new social image of the champion. It is admitted, even asserted, that the champion can no longer practise his or her sport without being 'prepared', no doubt psychologically, but one way or another essentially doped up to produce the required spectacle. Something the World Anti-Doping Agency (WADA), directly attached to the IOC, has implicitly recognized since it is close to authorizing corticosteroids in competition, to speed recovery from muscle fatigue; they are also effective painkillers, generating feelings of euphoria and power defying exhaustion. WADA has accordingly asked accredited test laboratories not to rate as positive 'samples found to contain corticosteroids in concentrations below 30 nanogrammes per millilitre' (*Libération*, 8 April 2005). Far from being put off by it, the public attitude to the champion's image and role in society has fastened on this new fact. The doped-up champion is a victim who ought to have the right to make or remake his own career.

The supporters play a role here too, one of considerable force in the acceptance of doping, which is perceived not as shameful but as an accomplishment whose defence has become almost respectable. So can we really identify a crisis in sport because of doping? And if we can, what sort of crisis is it? Is there a decline in the public popularity of doped-up champions or, on the contrary, a renewal of admiration? Since doping is officially banned, the current crisis implies a quasi-systematic surveillance of competitions, and their entrance into a legalistic domain.

Let us be clear at the outset that doping is not some regrettable or vexatious deviation from squeaky-clean origins, the result of an accidental encounter between the neutral athlete and dubious or illegal products. The doping phenomenon is not the outcome of an untoward or random contamination of pure, innocent, naive individuals by impure substances.

Secondly, we should treat doping in sport as a corollary of the development of competitive sport since the late nineteenth century. The real expansion of doping took place in the context of new national and international competitions. Of course, in the late nineteenth century, people did not use the products available in the early twenty-first. On the other hand, doping is today so widespread among athletes and players on every level that the 'savour' of the sporting exploit is inseparable from it: *sport would not exist without doping*. It appears that some youngsters with a talent for football have their performance boosted by steroids from the age of twelve or thirteen. And 'according to a specialized journal, the *British Journal of Sports Medicine*, more than one in a hundred French eleven-year-olds could be using substances to boost their performance' (*Le Monde*, 19 June 2007). The entire sporting institution is no longer just touched by doping, but literally invaded by it. Worse still, it makes a living out of it.

Thirdly, the real race is for a form of doping timed to deliver maximum performance at the right moment. Remember that sporting performance is inhuman by definition, an artificial construct involving the introduction of an external substance potentially dangerous to the body. What is globally seen as sporting performance is in total contradiction with the natural capacities of the body, even one transformed and modified over a thousand years. For the truth is that the body has undergone a slow but inexorable 'sportification' process. Current performances and records are the result of permanent doping of the sporting champ. The public is actually applauding 'cyborgs', whose bodies have been poisoned with undetectable chemical products. Apart from the classic amphetamines, human growth hormone (HGH), erythopoietin (EPO), testosterone and the anabolic steroid nandrolone, a recent arrival has been tetrahydrogestrinone (THG). This 'synthetic steroid was specially developed to evade anti-doping tests. Squarely in the frame is the US Balco laboratory and its boss, Victor Conte, who is believed to have offered the product to numerous athletes. THG is supposed to be an anabolizer, although this has not yet been proved. If such were the case, then its side-effects would be similar to those of other steroids.'

Entirely new substances have been appearing in the sporting field. Secretagogues are molecules that stimulate natural production of HGH; Vascular Endothelial Growth Factor (VEGF) helps to develop vascular tissue (more blood, more oxygen, so greater endurance); gene therapy and myostatin increase muscle mass by blocking resorption. Other magic potions are still at the experimental stage: HIF (Hypoxia Inducible Factor), a protein that helps counteract the effects of low oxygen levels, and now FibroGen's FG-2216, which helps increase oxygen carried by the blood, stimulating natural production of erythropoetin, increasing iron production and using it more efficiently. SARMS (Selective Androgen Receptor Moderators) are promising molecules that act like testosterone without its undesirable side-effects (facial and bodily hair growth, greasy skin, acne, pattern baldness and depression in men; masculinization including deepening of the voice, body and facial hair growth, irreversible enlargement of the clitoris and menstrual disruption in women, even after brief and limited use). Long-term heavy use of any sort of anabolic steroid can lead to increased or depleted sex drive, sleep apnoea, breathing problems, mood swings, aggression, painful and persistent erections, shrinkage of the testicles, enlarged prostate and the appearance of breasts in men. Large doses over long periods can cause liver damage with results ranging from jaundice to hepatitis, haemorrhage and cancer. All sporting champions risk serious psychic and physical health problems in later life, and some are heading for an early grave. Football players collapse on the field before the cameras; cyclists vanish more discreetly in mid-race or fail to awaken one morning; more and more athletes are dying young.

But what does doping really boil down to in the end? What is its place in relation to sport itself? We would dispute the widespread view of it as a perverse effect, a tragic phenomenon that appeared accidentally and partially infected sport, and that should be denounced and vigorously suppressed; no, it is wired directly into sport itself. In other words, *doping is not external to sport but has come to be its very basis.* As a result of the social value attributed to champions, doping has blossomed in the very heart of sport, filtering down from the professional level through the intermediate ranks to small local clubs. The infernal logic of the pursuit of records, performance and prowess drove sport to embrace the poison, led to the development of risky products that damage athletes and send them in increasing numbers towards an almost programmed death. So doping should not be seen as an aberration, , but recognized as the core, the deep framework of sport as it currently exists. From being a chronic but discreet presence – doping has always existed to a variable extent in sporting competitions, even during the ancient Greek Olympic Games – it has become *structural* in sport as it is now practised. Modern sport today, without doping, could not exist.

Conversely, any sporting events subjected to some level of drugs testing, announced in advance, are events without genuine performance; they thus become of limited interest to audiences, and are rewarded by the media with scornfully sketchy coverage. The best response they can hope for is a vaguely indulgent smile. A men's 100-metre sprint in a time of 10.1 or 10.2 seconds is hardly thought worth watching (the standing world record is still Usain Bolt's 9.58 seconds, set in Berlin on 16 August 2009). Television has underscored these differences between levels of competition. Through its close-ups, slow-motion replays and the like, TV spectators over time have absorbed visually what constitutes a 'real' performance, a fast time, an exceptional jump, the possibility of a record. Television in this way has trained viewers to make sense of the performance on which the whole spectacle, with its emotional charge, is hinged. Once again, then: without amazing performances or better still a record – preferably a world record – the spectacle does not exist, and public interest in sport declines considerably. To obtain records, doping has therefore become obligatory, necessary, the only solution; with doping, sport as it really exists can take full flight. By incorporating doping into its competitive logic, sport on an unearthly scale and in a different dimension is taking shape everywhere, and reproducing itself as the only reality: a reality that exists in a globalized form channelled by television. So that the next few years promise something better than a rapprochement between sport and doping: one foresees their probable osmosis, in a new cycle of competitions accepted as one-off spectaculars.

Against this already sombre background, moreover, new contradictions potentially damaging to sport have arisen, casting doubt on its long-term survival. One such contradiction, far from resolved, is this: doping has certainly given the development of sport a new momentum with higher speeds, dazzling performance levels and the possibility of new records. But in the process, doping flies in the face of the values with which sport has always been associated: health, eternal youth, humanism, beauty ... and therefore has to be seen as a questionable aspect of competitive sport in its present form. It has the effect of enforcing a rapid turnover of champions, who are now starting to succeed one another at what might appropriately be called record speed. Apart from that, doping and the accelerating rhythms of competitive sport are leading to more and more injuries. 'Sporting damage' is a widespread and serious problem among athletes. Top-level athletes are only competitive – called 'active' these days – in the periods between injuries. They spend a lot of time recovering, as doping, to put it mildly, has done little to improve their natural bodily balance and resilience.

But doping does help to keep sport going, constantly recasting its reality by linking it to the idea of continuous human progress, of constant change and improvement towards an imagined, essential ideal. Sport generates and permanently renews its stocks of athletes ready for anything. However, this permanent and continuous development is slowing, and will at some as yet undetermined moment be stopped altogether, by the impassable horizon of sporting performance: the singularity of the body as an ontological barrier. Doped up or not, it must eventually reach its limits in space and time. Those limits are already looming in some sports whose asymptotic curve of records is almost flat, demanding increasingly fine measurements of distance or time: millimetres, micrometres, hundredths or thousandths of a second (skiing, sprints and distance races, swimming, Formula 1 ...). When the next record – a mainspring of competitive sport – is definitively beyond reach, what significance will attach to the sporting spectacle of athletes who, however enhanced, are no longer capable of repeating their exploits time and again?

Doping in sport is among the few contemporary phenomena that make it possible even to imagine an infinite progression. It has fostered this illusion of continuous upward progress in the setting of new records. Nevertheless, doping was long regarded by the sporting world as a form of cheating, to be deplored or condemned. Of course, the inherent qualities of the products and techniques used are also expected to 'improve', to maintain the upward record curve. So, at the heart of sport, and woven into the very logic of sporting competition, lies the contradiction between the 'positive' aspects of doping (better performances, more spectacle) and its 'negative' character: cheating, the sufferings that have to be endured, and death.

However, these two aspects of a single process are not antagonistic; weaving around each other, they seem to be opposed but are really complementary, feeding off each other, boosting each other alternately to mutate into a new and improved contradiction. The contradiction ensuing from doping in sport expresses what Karl Marx, in a different time and context, called the 'unity of opposites'. The contradiction of doping in sport is thus never stationary or paralysed; it is woven into a series of other, shifting contradictions, on which the new mode of sporting production is being assembled, with doping as its lubricant. In team sports without measurable 'performance' or records – football, rugby, most ball games – generalized doping seems to have a 'levelling' effect on the teams, but this is another illusion: there will always be sportsmen less doped up, or better 'prepared', than others. The same applies to athletic events, where there will always be a winner and a trail of losers. Today's athletes, across all disciplines, run like hares, are never out of breath, recover from their superhuman efforts within minutes of the end of the race or game; most are impressively muscle-bound. So the very evolution of that first contradiction sets off new ones, superseding the old ones and giving birth to yet others in their turn.

The second thing to understand about the contradiction implicit in doping is its mediating character. Doping *mediates* between sport and competition, or records. It is with the support of that mediation, or even by using it as a foundation, that sport constitutes itself through a dialectical process: permanent deployment of its opposites and resolution of those opposites, in an unending rotation. The very logic of competitive sport pushes it permanently towards doping, while, in the same movement, doping pushes a lot of individuals towards sport, while ruining or destroying the health of sportsmen … Faced with this horror show, 'The important thing at present,' as Marx wrote (in a rather different connection, of course), 'is to take note of the existence of these contradictions' (*Grundrisse*).

We cannot but wonder how the doping question will be resolved. Will the practice diminish as a result of legislation and sanctions, or will we see its rapid increase and/or integration as an element indissociable from competitive sport? In the current phase of expansion and media exposure of the use of doping products in all sports, it seems unlikely that doping will disappear in the short or medium term. Most sportsmen, for their part, still deny their dependence on drugs, while appealing for endorsement from their supporters and a public already won over to their cause. Athletes known to be doped up have never been so popular; any who die are swiftly labelled martyrs to the cause of sport ... So, although it is unlikely to disappear in the near future, doping could well develop in a direction enabling it to act on a more fundamental level, through a possible mutation of bodily structure. 'Superseding' the current doping contradiction will mean putting together a different body, mutating it by surgically grafting parts of limbs, tissues or muscles, or better still by acting on living tissue at the cellular level, modifying a DNA whose entire code is now known. To manufacture another body, to make available to sport a new, renewable body, must be the dream of many a sorcerer's apprentice. Will we soon be cheering on genetically modified athletes? Current advances in biomedical research encourage the notion that a new sporting body, technologically and chemically 'race-tuned' in the factory, could soon be unveiled. The possibility exists that sometime in the twenty-first century sport will 'absorb' doping, by producing a new species of sporting mutants. For the moment, let us note that doping is consubstantial with sport. Drugs and sport are now indissociably linked. *Doping constitutes sport in its totality and as a totality.*

In light of the above, one is tempted to speculate on the role of sport itself as a drug – the modern hard drug addicting countless millions worldwide. The advance towards the fabrication of a chemicals-stuffed *homo sportivus* is accompanied by an escalating interest in sports stars themselves on the part of fans and sports-lovers. These supporters do not call for less cheating in sport; they are not embarrassed by the plethora of sport, nor do they see doping as shameful. But they are disappointed by the feebleness of sporting offerings in terms of record times, exceptional feats and incomparable spectacle. Most of all they are disappointed by the fact that sport is still not quite continuous, not uninterruptedly fed through the televisual filter to screens stretching from horizon to horizon and penetrating the smallest crannies of everyday life; they resent the fact that sport has not yet replaced every single activity of the individual, whether intellectual, artistic or other. For such is the *totalitarian character* of sport, driven to substitute itself for every other living thing and achieve total hegemony. Sport certainly does resemble an addiction in society, a drug consumed continuously and with eager enjoyment by large and growing numbers of individuals: sportsmen, fans, spectators and television viewers. People who can never live fulfilling lives, being in the grip of that enslaving power known as sport.

10. THE GLOBALIZATION OF SPORT THROUGH DOPING

The fall of the Berlin Wall in 1989 contained the promise of a benign globalization. It had seemed too much to hope for, given the rapid development of a pure, hard-core capitalism crossed with a mafia-like socio-political order in the former strongholds of 'real socialism'. But in the East, in just a few years and almost without violence, an empire collapsed into itself without outside intervention. Something that had seemed indestructible – a vast society spread over a gigantic territory with its military, its police, nuclear technology and so on – splintered apart in quite a short time. Something that had been thought eternal fell to pieces without a sign of regret from a society willing to accept a Western economy, amid a new profusion of merchandise now being supplemented from the heart of the former Soviet empire and its satellites.

The abrupt implosion of the so-called socialist regimes liberated the consumers' thirst for goods and their overwhelming desire to embrace capitalist values and to sweep away anything that might still recall the former system. Great hordes of people rushed to satisfy their long-frustrated desire to consume, flocking into the inviting supermarkets, immense hangars stuffed with goods available to all. On returning home, sated and somewhat nauseated by these visits to the new temples of consumer debauchery, people slumped in front of a mind-sapping screen. Slowly the countries of the former Soviet bloc were liquidating their past, leaving a clear field for the new values and the inexhaustible availability of consumer products, from the basic to the sophisticated. The ex-communists – party chiefs, members of the different police bodies, patented bureaucrats and so on – learned a good deal from their Western counterparts and incorporated most of the values of a system whose essentials they adopted with panache, while developing or maintaining their own way of doing things with a certain crafty knowhow. For it is well known that while the dominant system is capitalist (generalized and violent competition, obsession with profits, limitless market expansion, crises galore, warmongering …), the new businessmen of the former Soviet rampart were able to entrench their existing methods in readiness for the new markets starting to appear.

Now we see them taking an interest in sporting affairs, starting with British football: the owner of the Chelsea team is Roman Abramovich, a Russian oil magnate. Russians, but not only Russians, are coming to 'old Europe' to take up powerful positions in the world of finance, and currently in sport. A US billionaire, Malcolm Glazer – the 278th richest person in the world – holds 28 per cent of the shares in Manchester United, and today controls 57 per cent of them. Glazer also owns one of the better American football franchises, the Tampa Bay Buccaneers. Other English teams part- or majority-owned by US citizens are Aston Villa (Randy Lerner); Sunderland, Liverpool, and Arsenal (bought in 2011 by Stan Kroenke). Manchester City belongs to the half-brother of the Emir of Abu Dhabi, Sheikh Mansour; Fulham belongs to an Egyptian; Birmingham City to Hong Kong millionaire Carson Yeung, and Blackburn to the Rao brothers, Indian owners of the Venky's chicken processing conglomerate. Apart from all that, links between high-level sport and organized crime are thought to be growing closer.

What is the significance of all this to sport in the context of the current globalization? Where the Eastern countries had achieved something of a head start, in the areas of intensive training and medical follow-up thanks to the massive doping of their athletes, the West did not have a lot to teach them. The end of the Cold War had made it possible to appreciate the full inhumanity of the conditions under which athletes had been trained, particularly in that military-sporting barracks that was the GDR. Inhumanity is not too strong a word, with athletes, women especially, being subjected to 'medical' experimentation for many years, compelled to absorb high doses of doping products often without their consent or knowledge. The consequences of this *state criminality* were often appalling: gross weight gain, amenorrhea (absence of menstruation) in very young girls, long-lasting or permanent injuries; in other words seriously hazardous treatment, destruction of the body in fact, by sport becoming a form of more or less 'soft' torture. Longer-term effects could be more terrible still: bone malformations, development of multiple cancers, premature death ... In this area, a country like the GDR had a lead of several lengths over the capitalist West which was still in its sports-doping infancy, even though a few champions were known to make heavy use of the products.

At that time, cycling offered the most favourable environment for experimentation. Among hundreds of other examples, some may recall the French cyclists Jacques Anquetil and Laurent Fignon, who both died of cancer in their early fifties, and the British racer Tom Simpson who died of heat exhaustion during a race, ascending Mont Ventoux after taking amphetamines. One of the paradoxes of the Western camp, so soon after the 'liberation' of the so-called communist countries, the countries of 'real socialism', was its attempt to emulate the Eastern model in its approach to sports organization. The set-up was not directly imported from the East, but copied in its general orientation and structure: the quest for bodily performance, experiments on human guinea-pigs, institutionalized doping ... The fall of the Berlin Wall liberated the West from its 'inhibitions' on the limits of sports training, leading to the development of a system equivalent to that of the former Eastern countries. Massive doping could now become the foundation of a globalized sporting edifice.

So even as former Eastern bloc champions were revealing the sordid details of their youth spent largely in sports doctors' laboratories during the 1970s, doping on a grand scale (both quantitative and qualitative) was being developed in the West, and increasingly seen as normal and commonplace by sponsors seeking 'dazzling' and 'unprecedented' performances in most sports, beginning with cycling (Tour de France, Giro d'Italia), going on to athletics (Olympic Games) and finally overtaking football, to become standard practice in European clubs. Every sporting discipline – tennis, baseball, swimming – ended by acknowledging their broad complicity or intimate involvement with doping. The need to be on top form for important international meetings launched a mad doping race, well under way in time for the Olympic Games in China. Despite the secretive nature of the People's State, the US Drug Enforcement Agency (DEA) in 2007 revealed that it had closed down '26 illegal laboratories making anabolic androgenic steroids [and] that all these laboratories were being supplied from 37 factories in China. "We found in the end that 99.9 per cent of the anabolic steroids present in the US came from China"' (*Le Monde*, 25 September 2007).

These data suggest that the current globalization, of which sport is an essential vector – economic, social and ideological – is not being implemented in one direction only, or by a single route from West to East. The globalization process is far more complex than has been made out. *Sporting globalization is being carried on the back of doping globalization.* Pioneered by East European sorcerers' apprentices perfecting new laboratory 'super-rats' for the great sporting circus, and now spearheaded by China, globalized doping has come back in finished form to a sporting world now structurally entangled with a 'scientific medicine' focused mainly on the production and consumption of performance-enhancing substances. The model of sports doping, today almost accepted as normal, originated in Eastern Europe and was then globalized, spreading westward to reach the US. The US certainly produces some exceptional performances nowadays, despite reverses such as the notorious Balco scandal. The Bay Area Laboratory Cooperative was discovered to be producing illegal steroids and supplying them to a number of champions (now disgraced). These included Dwain Chambers, Michelle Collins, Kelli White, Tim Montgomery and of course Marion Jones, the 'golden girl' of US athletics, who was forced to return her Olympic medals.

It may not be recalled that in the early 1970s the Soviet Union had attempted to justify scientifically the unscrupulous race for records and quest for enhanced 'performance', referring to the programme to produce a bodily abnormal human as 'anthropomaximology'. This shamelessly scientistic neologism, reeking of Stalinist mould, seemed to show what sort of price the men of steel were ready to exact from their future champions. At any rate, a good number of medal-winners from the East owed their success to a state enterprise for the synthetic manufacture of athletes' bodies. Recently, after the discovery of Stasi documents showing that the blanket doping policy had been taken over and run by the state, compensation was granted to 167 former GDR athletes of the estimated 10,000 officially doped between 1970 and the late 1980s.

Today, of course, the same sort of thing is woven into the great sports enterprise the West has become along with its immediate fringes, where increasing numbers of East European athletes (foot-ballers, cyclists, tennis players) are starting to show up in clubs and teams. But it is China, the world's great workshop, that has become the obvious centre for the manufacture, distribution and consumption of doping products; and China has become the sporting nation par excellence. So China will be preparing its new chemical athletes discreetly, in absolute secrecy, in state training camps.

The set-up sounds strangely similar to what one would have expected in the former GDR.

> Four thousand sports schools, 212 elite boarding schools, robust methods, training to the point of exhaustion: China loves sport and medals. ... After the economic miracle, the world's workshop wants to prevail as a factory making champions. ... The frenetic growth of red capitalism is answered – echoed – by the exaltation of performance and the regimentation of amateurs. ... At the top of the pyramid, between 100 and 150 champions will get the bulk of the sports preparation budget for the 2008 Olympics ... The creed of performance at all costs touches on a third taboo, that of doping. As the Olympics draw nearer, China is finding it difficult to avoid suspicion. ... Last year, senior sports staff in Liaoning province, a breeding-ground of Chinese champions, were purged following a second testosterone doping affair. In 2000, on the eve of the Sydney Games, China had to withdraw 27 athletes from its delegation. (*Le Figaro*, 8 August 2007.)

11. THE GLOBALIZATION OF SPORT AND THE SPORTING MODE OF PRODUCTION

The globalization of sport means not only the territorial and institutional extension of the expanding market for sport, but also the development of a new mode of production for a new type of merchandise, namely, top-class athletes able to ratchet up records and performances of every sort. This mode of production in its globalized form culminates in the Olympics or other major international competitions, and rests on several solid foundation points: a state sports structure developed more or less independently by each country, but based on the same structural model; an economy directly centred on sport (with its own capital, markets, budgets and businessmen), and the framework of scientific and technological organization (with its planetary networks, stateless athletes and worldwide doping). While the nation remains the preferred setting and expression for sports organization, sport can only be fully deployed when globalized.

Football has been one of the main vectors of this globalization, being a synthesis of the new elements capitalism can deploy today: the spirit of enterprise, of the successful entrepreneur, allied with a capacity to communicate on all fronts – through the pervasive power of television (dominated by the likes of Berlusconi, Bouygues and Murdoch) and latterly the Internet – and the probability of prompt financial returns. That seems to be the new configuration of capitalism: nothing lasting, stable or solid, rather the flash and glitter of the instantaneous, the violence of unfettered, untamed enterprise, the grandeur of the improvised. Sport thus constitutes a model in miniature of capitalism, or rather the reduction of capitalism to its most powerful vector. For what holds good for sport now covers all social activities across the planet. As Ernest Mandel indicates,

The development of the capitalist mode of production implies the generalization of commodity production for the first time in mankind's history. This production no longer embraces merely luxury products, the surplus of foodstuffs or other goods of current consumption, metals, salt and other products indispensable for maintaining and extending the social surplus product. Everything that is the object of economic life, everything that is produced is henceforth a commodity: all foodstuffs, all consumer goods, all raw materials, all means of production, including labour-power itself.

In parallel with the rapid emergence of sport as a specific mode of production, a new globalized ideology has arisen and taken root, that of the self-made sportsman, living proof that sport can bring social success; that you can be born in a slum and yet make it through sport.

The globalized new man resembles the predominant sporting type as seen in the advertisements that serve to bolster his image: highly enterprising, not particularly virtuous, cynical when necessary, coolly efficient; physically, bronzed and beautiful and often compared to wild animals (tiger, panther, gazelle …). Thanks to the wide diffusion of this positive image, the sports figure effectively represents everything the market can handle in its vast consumer warehouses, and in parallel irrigates the whole great global neoliberal ideology. It is impossible to miss the irresistible power with which sport is diffused in all its forms and in every way, direct and indirect, like a veritable pandemic: passed on by suppliers and manufacturers of every sort, through all outlets across the planet, projected through the plethora of screens. The globalization of state economies is being structured and deployed in measurable part through sport. While football remains the main vector of propagation at present, there are a number of sub-vectors with similar economic, political and ideological contaminative power such as rugby, athletics, basketball, tennis, golf, or Formula 1, but diffused on a smaller scale, more slowly or via different channels. Some of these may fancy their chances of replacing football, should football ever falter in its role of prime disseminator of globalized sporting ideology.

Sporting globalization is closely entangled with tourist globalization, that other leisure activity of the mobile masses. From the 1930s onward in Western Europe, alongside the idea of a 'leisure civilization' and the advent of paid holidays, mass leisure development policies were launched including the encouragement of sport from a young age. Such policies durably impregnated the public mind with the alleged virtues of sport: health, youth, happiness …

The fact is that the sporting institution is emerging as one of the most powerful worldwide organizations in relation to the system of planetary economic exchange, with its heavyweight, overlapping control and management instruments (UN, UNESCO, ILO, WTO, IMF, etc.). Like these other international institutions, sport is centred on an organizational and administrative model controlling and supervising a gigantic apparatus of technical and technological output, communication and distribution of products. Since the end of the nineteenth century, with the gradual establishment of its own channels, networks and structures (ranging from the IOC to football and athletics clubs via a range of federations), and the development of a colossal market with budgets comparable to those of several Western states, the sporting institution has steadily developed and consolidated itself as a specific mode of production. Alongside the capitalist mode of production, in which capital appropriated labour under technical conditions brought into existence by its own historical processes, a sporting mode of production evolved, in which capital appropriated the body to make it into a winning machine, an essential gear train in the apparatus for producing surpluses. Eventually, sport became as it were a dominant model for a mode of production. The two modes are not antagonistic or in competition. They cohabit, connect and combine; in a word they cooperate, while still developing in autonomous fashion.

The sporting mode of production does not involve the transformation of isolated into social labour so as to render it more profitable, in the traditional sense of Marx's analysis of the capitalist mode of production. But sport has certainly created its own class system, with a 'proletariat' and a 'bourgeoisie'. An athlete or player can start at the wide base of the social pyramid as an aspiring semi-amateur and become the sort of professional we all recognize as a star, one of a handful of individuals at the summit. Similarly, a distinct sporting bourgeoisie runs the business side of sport, as equipment manufacturers, club administrators, agents and fixers in the immense transfer market, or staff of national and international federations and sporting bodies. Like workers and employees, high-level athletes sell their labour power as a commodity on a highly competitive market, but on an altogether different price scale. The role of unpaid labour is also important in sport. It is sometimes needed at big sporting events when the organizers and police are unsure of maintaining security, inside and outside the stadium, or when stars are asked to appear at enormous gatherings of various sorts. The aediles of sport rely heavily on this element of non-remunerated labour to build up, at minimal expense, an already considerable added value.

Because it is characterized by its rapid globalization through the processes analysed above, the sporting mode of production plays a full part in the overturning or mutation of former modes (artisanal, feudal or capitalist). Sport has neither broken these up nor dissolved into them, but has absorbed them as components into its own structure, so that within the sporting mode of production, other former modes connect and interlace as shifting entities, strata or layers of an overall process. Vestiges of feudalism may be recognized, say, in the forms of serfdom imposed on young football hopefuls in some African countries, alongside the presence of the most naked capitalism in the form of continuous market growth, accelerated robotization of athletes in the grip of appropriated medical technologies, an immense sporting reserve army, a sporting proletariat and even a lumpenproletariat.

In other words, the sporting mode of production draws together old and new modes of exploitation from the traditional and more recent sectors of agriculture, industry, new cutting-edge technologies and communications (television, Internet) and unifies them into a 'superior' entity – but on the basis of the development each of these modes of production had achieved during their separate histories. Sport is tending to assemble, amalgamate and then fuse all these productive sectors, and to become itself the omnipotent new mode of production at the leading edge of a new, different system.

This sporting mode of production is producing a quantitative leap in the extension (globalization and homogenization) of the market through the proliferation of sporting commodities in circulation or on sale both direct (equipment, sporting goods, materials and accessories of all types) and indirect (television retransmission rights for competitions), and is encouraging fierce rivalry between the European nations, in order to retain control of markets and products still external to Europe. Hence the commercial preference for any sport-related product made in the US or China.

12. THE SHOW STADIUM

At the heart of the globalized media apparatus, where throbs the spectacle of sport, there lies an edifice of a unique sort, instantly recognizable from its shape despite a measure of historical evolution. The stadium is a form of architecture that is utterly specific, both a visually imposing structure and one that imposes a vision. The modern stadium resembles a monumental feat by reason, among other things, of its uncommon scale; it soars above the surrounding buildings, to be visible from a distance and sufficiently overbearing at close quarters. Inside its enclosure, spectators can see and hear the sporting spectacle in the best possible way, and watch important moments replayed on screens placed over the stands or over the curved ends of the stadium. Finally, the stadium is integral to the universal diffusion of the match or competition as it is retransmitted into millions of homes by television.

The stadium thus helps to distort reality by facilitating close focus on a fierce sporting struggle between competitors ambitious for victory, visually projecting the reality of a miniaturized world dominated by a gigantic sports show stretched out to blanket the planet. This distortion of reality is accentuated by the invasion of the stadium space with different-sized screens showing the athletes' play from angles unavailable to the spectators, replaying crucial moves in slow motion and close-up, rerunning 'technical' feats on a rolling loop, and so on. The stadium is basically a high-output image mill, sleekly functionalized and rationalized. From that central hub, images of sport are beamed into every place on earth where there is a television receiver.

The stadium's architecture thus takes the ideal form of a compact building providing a visual matrix for the projection of this fountain of images. As we have seen, the form is perfectly adapted to the perception and reception of the sporting spectacle by Elias Canetti's 'mass in a ring', and for its further reception by another, dispersed mass of spectators, isolated from one another but brought together by the sporting spectacle in a highly susceptible 'emotional community' (Max Weber). More generally, all available spaces, private and public – stadium, houses, streets, parks and squares – are invaded and sometimes swamped by an audio-visual system geared to the impregnation of individual consciousness, because all the technology deployed is subordinate to that system. In the stadium, the sights and sounds of the spectacle are unleashed together in a common setting out of the 'stagnant mass' (Canetti) of spectators, and broadcast simultaneously into the homes of television spectators.

The alienation that then occurs in the stadium derives from the colonization of the audio-visual panorama, or rather the extreme enfeeblement of the visual, by the mediation of screens. The totality of the visual package being organized in the stadium – what is seen by the spectators, what is generated by cameras, etc. – is reduced to an abstraction, or 'alienated', because individuals are thus dispossessed of their senses. The reality inside the tight frame of the stadium is based on reorganization of the aural and visual environment for purposes of media effectiveness; it acts on the whole body, the whole mass of bodies, subjecting them to abstraction or sensory alienation, taking them 'out of themselves'. And the latest generation of stadiums, exemplified by the Dallas Cowboys' stadium built in collaboration with Sony Electronics, have inaugurated a comprehensively audio-visual environment with a giant 49m x 8m screen suspended over the centre of the pitch, flanked by two others each measuring 30m x 12m. A production and mixing studio allows spectators to witness and overhear conversations between the players, or between players and trainers; twenty large screens greet spectators in the approaches to the stadium, and 3,000 flat LCD screens keep them immersed wherever they may be inside it, from the VIP boxes or lobbies to the retail zones, corridors and lavatories.

And that is not all. Anyone entering the stadium with the latest must-have communication gadget has wireless Internet access. Using WiseDV's new LVIS miniature video apparatus, stadium spectators (but also TV viewers and even video spectators) can watch replays from six different angles in fast or slow motion on 4-inch hand-held screens, at the same time as watching live or broadcast the feats of their favourite players. So the new-style spectators will be able to edit games for themselves, using state-of-the-art image technology that gives access to live transmission of the action with manual control of the image, instant slow-motion replays, instant access to statistics, simultaneous viewing of other sporting events, live commentary from linked radio stations, and so on.

The size and placing of the screens in this latest type of stadium nevertheless plays a part in blurring the border between reality and representation; image and reality are superimposed and overlaid to create a fuzzy overall picture; the screens have no surrounding 'frames', so that the image can bleed into the background of massed real spectators. The screen image seems more real, as if the image were emerging from the stadium backdrop, as if the stadium itself were a sort of screen. More generally, the current perceived reality of sport is substantially composed of images of sport, and is thus extensively defined by these jumps and cuts, in a feverish shuffling of reality and representation. The stadium's strength is that it backs up the initial, observed reality – the sporting competition taking place before the spectators' eyes, unfiltered by screens – with a reality retransmitted through screens inside the stadium and of course outside it in people's homes. That is the intrinsic power of stadiums invaded by screens: to blur the outlines, to blend the real with the fictional, to confuse reality with representation, to get them so entangled that no one can tell them apart any more.

THE 'SCREEN-STADIUM' AND THE BODY

The aspect of seeing that concerns us here is primarily the question of visualization. Not what is seen directly, but how and through what it is seen, through what mechanism sight is directed, or controlled; what is the technology that takes possession of the eye and the gaze. The stadium is that extraordinary machine, not just passively vis-ualized but actively visualizing: a seeing machine. Festooned with screens of every size, the stadium has become more than a recepta-cle for traditional and more modern media (radio, TV, Internet). It is a medium in its own right which, combined with sport – with its necessary visualization – engenders a radically new space-time. The deployment of a system of interactive media, one producing the other, one modifying the other, thus has 'its magnetic or attractive force [because it] values that constant – and insidious – shuttling back and forth between reality and fiction, between representation of the world and recreation of worlds, between "objectivization" of the real and symbolic organization of the chaos of the event'. This occurs most especially in the stadium, a junction point of numerous media and itself the leading medium for sport as spectacle.

But when we are so closely absorbed by the image of sport, are we still in a stadium? And when at home, are we just in front of the television, or are we somehow in the stadium? Reality has overtaken fiction. The stadium is no longer only a place furnished with ever more numerous and gigantic screens; television is no longer that ultimate screen in front of which hundreds of millions of individuals sprawl, their gaze captured and as if mesmerized by the sporting spectacle. The whole stadium has metamorphosed into a screen, an *immense screening mechanism* on which is fixed the blinded gaze of the spectators, 'emptied' of the sense of sight, a gaze that has been (as it were) filleted of the capacity for scrutiny and enquiry. Paradox is still there in taking support from the screen, from the lack of depth, the wafer thinness of that device giving the illusion of depth: but a depth that clings within the sole frame of the stadium, its geometric space.

The real power of the stadium, its extreme attraction, no longer resides in the multitude of screens placed everywhere. It resides in the manner of screening the stadium presents in its totality, in this contamination of the collective imagination through the screens deployed inside and outside the stadium. Jean Baudrillard in his day understood this radical metamorphosis:

We lived once in a world where the realm of the imaginary was governed by the mirror, by dividing one into two, by theatre, by otherness and alienation. Today that realm is the realm of the screen, of interfaces and duplication, of contiguity and networks. … We draw ever closer to the surface of the screen; our gaze is, as it were, strewn across the image. … It is invariably a tele-image – an image located at a very special distance which can only be described as unbridgeable by the body.' ('Xerox and Infinity'.)

That enabled Baudrillard to associate the screen 'with a form of frozen otherness, of confiscated otherness, perhaps ideal otherness, like that of the Ideal City where there is no one'. The stadium is a matter of real surfaces with fixed boundaries, screens like surfaces, detached from reality, but from a reality that asserts itself even in the screen and as a screen. These surfaces – these screens – help constitute the stadium while being detached fragments of it. Now it becomes clear how the specular diet of the body is so comprehensively mobilized throughout the media-stadium. It is inside the stadium, that place of experiment, that the body undergoes a profound change with the reduction of its five senses to that of sight alone, and in reified form. The body as a whole is subjected to a form of visual predation or one-way optical delirium by continuous and directed visual focus on the smallest sporting detail. The body of the spectator and TV spectator is also assigned its place: facing the game or facing one of the lavish profusion of screens.

24-HOUR SPORT: POPULAR AND MEDIA APPROVAL

The last football World Cup, held in South Africa in June and July 2010, which caused such torrents of ink to flow, showed the scale of consent to football on television. Thus for example, for the final between Spain and Holland, there were 700 million television spectators overall but 15.6 million Spanish ones – 86 per cent of the audience – and market share in Holland of over 90 per cent, not forgetting the 31 million Germans who tuned in to their lost semi-final. In the US, the African 'soccer' matches were getting a TV audience of 24.3 million. In France the audience remained quite high, despite or because of the drawn-out disgrace of the *Bleus* which kept a lot of fans on the edge of their seats. And despite the early defeat of the national team, all the French media – radio, TV and print – did well out of that World Cup, demonstrating that football is a formidable catalyst.

The figures speak for themselves; at least they seem to say what is important. Sport and more precisely international sporting events (Olympic Games, World Cups, continental cups in all major sports) and national ones (championships between city clubs) have been for forty years more mediatized than any other events.

'Sport programmes have achieved exceptional audiences this year, constantly exceeding previous limits, like the athletes who are also beating reputedly unreachable records', said Jacques Braun, vice-president of the ratings analysis company Eurodata TV Worldwide, at the launch of its 'Yearly Sport Key Facts 2010' report. For the Athens Olympic Games in 2004, what this meant was a TV audience of 3.9 billion, served by 300 channels retransmitted in 220 countries. Day and night, the broadcast of sporting events is more or less guaranteed by television on both public and private channels. What this demonstrates for our purposes is the centrality of sport's role in the media and the committed stance of the media in return, not just giving sporting events saturation coverage, but promoting them with all their might. Where one might still expect to see some competition between media, one sees instead a sort of syndicate bent on pledging continuity of sport across all the media. Of the current three and a half hours on average spent in front of the screen, most is given to sport. One notes too that news and current affairs programmes devote a large amount of airtime to sport, when not actually leading with some result useful for the maintenance or stiffening of collective narcissism ('France wins!' 'The Blues are back!' 'The nation is liberated!' 'Long live [Marseille football team] OM!').

THE ORIGINS OF SPORT IN ITS IMAGE

Aficionados of the moving image may be familiar with the name Étienne Jules Marey, one of whose pupils described him as an 'engineer of the living'. A doctor and physiologist, he was also a tinkerer of genius who devised a number of photographic inventions to help with his work. Marey took an early interest in the analysis of 'movement' and the representation of the 'machine-animal' in movement. 'He introduced a new language to describe the workings of the body, the language of time and motion', and is best remembered for inventing the chronophotographic gun (1882), a camera intended to capture movement and a precursor of the cinema which was born at the end of the nineteenth century, at the same time as the first modern Olympic Games. In Marey's contraption, the cylinder (of a revolver) was replaced by a fixed photographic plate, with a rotating slotted disc designed to act as a shutter. The plate was subsequently replaced with a moving strip of sensitized paper that stopped inter-mittently, like the film in a movie camera or projector. By 1893 he was able to project moving images.

'Shooting' without harming, Marey captured precious images that were to enter the heritage of world sport during the 1900 Paris Olympics, associated with the Exposition Universelle, two of the founding events of modernity. The images, original as they were, were fabricated in a 'theatre' or studio using a black background to capture movements in silhouette, in particular those specific to athletes. Their movements were broken down into a series of fixed images to identify the decisive phases. The same technique could be used with long jump, hurdling or a gymnast on the parallel bars; 'typical' bodily positions were thus frozen as a single image thought to represent normal human perception of the entire movement. Henri Bergson, a colleague of Marey in a research group at the Collège de France, systematized this by demonstrating the importance of the perceiving awareness: 'In just the same way the thousands of suc-cessive positions of a runner are contracted into one sole symbolic attitude, which our eye perceives, which art reproduces, and which becomes for everyone the image of a running man.'

Under Marey's leadership some fifty doctors and researchers established a sports study programme to analyse the physiological effects of sport and uncover the reasons for the perceived superiority of champions' bodies. This research would not have been possible without the invention of many ingenious photographic devices, which together amounted to a technological system for 'grasping' the body. By examining successive images of athletes' bodies in action, it was possible to isolate motions deemed redundant with a view to correcting them. This, combined with the study of mus-culature, led to better knowledge of the workings of the athlete's body for purposes of rectification or improvement, resulting in what might be called a sporting-aesthetic anthropometry. It is known that Marey's work had a strong influence on painters like Degas and on such neo-impressionists as Seurat and Signac, and can even be discerned in Duchamp's *Nude Descending a Staircase*.

However, Marey knew that while the body is the source of move-ment, it can also act as a brake. The need was felt to analyse athletes' bodies moving at full stretch, at speed, and thus their relation to time (or rather, lost time). A defective or inadequate musculature, like wasted effort caused by 'bad' habits of movement, could hold the body back from developing a perfect action. The athlete's body consequently became the object of experiment on the basis of the images. 'Marey perfected his physiological measurement techniques to establish a physiological time standard', because movement in his view was the product of two structuring dimensions, time and space. Bergson radicalized and theorized these experiments by showing that 'deconstruction of movement in spatialized time and discovery of the unknown language of the body's forces are the expression of the crisis of positivism at the turn of the century'. According to Bergson, the 'crisis of reality' lay in the scientific view of the world, in the fact that the temporalization of space and the spatialization of time were problems intrinsic to the system for perceiving quantification and abstraction. In any case, 'scientific' analysis of athletic movement through graphic inscription of its image, or the contiguity of successive images and the continuity in some sense of the frozen image, or the simulation of movement in an image, established from the start a demonstrable link between sport and image, encapsulated in their reciprocal emergence.

After the non-lethal photographic 'gun' which left its targets – birds being the first – unharmed, Marey further developed his experimental equipment by devising a 'physiological station' consisting of tracks, a black screen and a mobile 'darkroom' running on rails. It seems he wanted to get out of the laboratory into the light and fresh air, to study living beings. The station was based on two circular, concentric tracks, the outer one – for horses – 500 metres long, the inner one for human runners. The tracks were edged with a line of posts each of which emitted a signal when passed. In essence, these arrangements on a flat, bare circular ground (but scenically encircled by trees) enabled the speed of a running horse or man to be measured and recorded – terms that in this context assume their full importance – by means of visual and sound devices. Some of the station's features anticipated the modern stadium to a certain extent.

The layout of the station required a trolley to hold a moving darkroom, running on a straight rail spur perpendicular to the tracks (to photograph movement from different distances). At the other end of the spur, on the opposite side of the circular running tracks, was a camera obscura, essentially a three-sided structure painted black, with a black velvet curtain in front of the rear wall. A photographer was placed in the darkroom, communicating with an assistant through a loudspeaker. The runner or horse would be dressed in white, illuminated by bright sunlight, the contrast with the 'absolute blackness' of the camera obscura enabling images to be shot very rapidly even with the slow photosensitive plates or paper available at the time. To record the time dimension, a clockwork timing mechanism with a luminous dial was placed in frame. So the photographic images were not just fractions of space showing the runner immobilized in mid-movement, but 'temporalized' on the photographic strip itself with black and white marks. This was really the birth of a system of time measurement whose original object – the subsequent importance of which in the sporting imagination we all know – was timekeeping. The whole arrangement anticipated the system needed by a stadium for the spectacle to be able to 'take place', in the most literal sense of the expression.

Sport now embodies the drift to a worldwide synchronization of time, a globalized matching of socio-political rhythms to its own tempo and cadence. It is directly associated with a media-defined mode of production, whose matrix is composed of images. Sport possesses a time of its own, marked by the supposedly steady fall of records and made visible by a globalized image distribution system. The theoretical task now, it would seem, is not to analyse sport as it appears in the glare of the media floodlights, but as a medium in its own right, the world's biggest medium, a spectacular screen-form on the scale of the planet. Sport may now project torrents of information that saturate time and space, but it also constitutes a unique news system in its own right. The important thing is not what the press, radio or television say about sport, but that the sporting ideology should be pumped through these multiple channels in a continuous flow of images. We are not just witnessing an increasing mediatization of sport, but mediatization deployed – *decreed* – by sport itself, in whose influence the media is steeped through and through.

13. THE POWER OF IMAGES

MEDIATIZED SPORT, SPORTIFIED MEDIA

Thoughtful analyses by the philosopher Günther Anders help to confirm that we are witnessing a globalized unification of human rhythms brought about by sport retransmitted by television. Images of sport are not simple images, and their retransmission is steeped in their ontological ambiguity. The broadcast events are present and absent, real and apparent, there and not there, because they are *shadows*. The power of sport resides in the infinite multiplication of the image in sport, and the image of sport as the image of what the world would like to be. The perpetual visualization of sport is the magical dimension of this globalization through images, the passion for sport universalized by the passion for the image, or 'iconomania'. The image in sport answers a form of repetition compulsion (in football, for example, every goal in every game is shown live, then in slow motion, then from different camera angles, in a loop unfolding ad infinitum). This has the effect of neutralizing all sense of time, trampling its measure underfoot: a random fibrillating rhythm, haste followed by sudden, syncope-like interruption, stopped dead and jerking forward, a rhythm that literally invades that of the human body and takes it over ... for sport must be lived. We find here the phenomenon of 'reproduction' that Walter Benjamin raised in a different context.

> In great ceremonial processions, giant rallies and mass sporting events, and in war, all of which are now fed into the camera, the

masses come face to face with themselves. This process, whose significance need not be emphasized, is closely bound up with the development of reproduction and recording technologies. In general, mass movements are more clearly apprehended by the camera than by the eye … That is to say that mass movements, and above all war, are a form of human behavior especially suited to the camera.

Only recently, two patented representatives of the historiography of sport noted with unfeigned pleasure that 'the history of sport and that of the mass media are experiencing a concomitant development, very little remarked upon. … Sport and media are working in concert towards the constitution of a mass culture which they are helping to shape, to modify, to spread, by way of radical technical innovations, new ways of mounting spectacles and talking about them, and inverted relations with the public authorities.' Perhaps 'culture' is too high-flown a term for what we understand today by the terms 'sport' and 'media'; 'culture industry' in Adorno's sense seems nearer the mark for this chapter, which concerns a general movement involving both sport and the media, and more than their association their interaction, interdependence and even entanglement.

It is well known that the rapid development of sport throughout the twentieth century was boosted by increasingly numerous and effective mass media: the written press, then the radio, followed by cinema, television and now the Internet mediated by screens large and small, on computers, tablets and mobile telephones as well as in public places – stadiums, city squares – and private homes, but nowadays increasingly carried on the body in a small format and consulted at all times. Siegfried Kracauer noticed which way the wind was blowing in the early 1930s:

> … those sporting events that spring up with an obstinacy that verges on monotony. … Everywhere in Germany, in the US, in England, and always amid an enormous crowd of the enthusiastic masses, there take place in the same settings football matches, motorcycle or horse races of which we are never spared the filmed highlights. These stereotyped sporting shots, which we know before we see them, exist without the slightest doubt not just to

satisfy the specialized interests of the public, but also to strengthen this attitude which prompts the disturbing exaggerations of sport.

In 1933 Goebbels considered radio 'the most modern and the most important tool imaginable for influencing the masses [and] impregnating people so thoroughly with the intellectual currents of our time that no one will be able to escape'. And in 1936, during the Berlin Olympics, 'the public was able to discover television for the first time: around a hundred and fifty thousand spectators were able to see the competitions live through collective receivers'. The Berlin Games also saw the first live television broadcasts of sporting competition. 'More than forty-one national radio broadcasting companies also covered the event, giving it an extraordinary worldwide audience, while nearly 100 stations transmitted the Games in the US alone, on the CBS and NBC networks.'

The Nazification of the German people was consolidated through the radio system in the development of programmes that avoided dullness, monotony and wordiness because then, Goebbels thought, 'people understand the intention and are put off.' Contrary to widespread belief, radio and TV, like sport and the 1936 Olympics, were not 'used' by the Nazi regime and were not 'corrupted' by the noxious system, but *developed in company* with it. Goebbels again recommended that television should 'offer an intelligent and psychologically adept blend of incitement, relaxation and entertainment. ... Very special attention needs to be given here to relaxation and entertainment, because the great majority of listeners ... aspire to find real relaxation and rest during their few hours of tranquillity and idleness.'

The historic promotion of sport by the media, which also helped to promote and popularize new sports (skiing, tennis, basketball, rugby), sometimes with changes to some of their rules, regulation dress or technologies (invention of the tie-break, permission for colourful clothing, alterations to the construction or colour of balls ...), is repaid by promotion of the media by sport, or even their *fusion* in a new and original entity: the *sport-spectacle* or *show-sport*. Sport may still be impossible without the media, but the media for their part are heavily infected with sport, colonized by the size of the sporting territory and the amount of daily space and airtime it consumes. In the era of mass media and mass sport, both sport and media have left the strict confines of their respective fields to engender, in what has become a synchronized move, an unprecedented, irresistible attractive power, able rapidly to seize and direct the consciousness of an immense multitude while shaping it to a certain worldview presented as fresh and new. The very scale of mass assent to the sporting spectacle is achieved on the basis of that coming together, that concordance or congruence between media in perpetual technical evolution but increasingly individualized or singularized, and consumption of competitive sport which congregates crowds of considerable size, and unites hordes of unleashed individuals. What the new world show-sport order – the fusion of sport and media in an unprecedented amalgam – seems to be proposing is nothing short of *reformatting* the world; or rather, the *projection* of a world external to life as it is experienced, one where the difference between living reality and its representation is permanently blurred; in a sense a sort of horizon, no longer unreachable, but brought as close as possible to the eye short of actually poking it out.

14. A STANDARDIZED AESTHETIC

In parallel with this vast planetary imaging process focused on the sporting phenomenon (television, cinema, advertising, newspapers, magazines, Internet), a major substitution is taking place. Art, as the main product of the imagination or as visualized thought, and games as free enjoyment of the human body, are being tendentiously supplanted by sport in the role of sole creative activity, the sole theatre of permanently visualized invention and pleasure. The instinct for play is being taken over and destroyed by the sporting reality principle, making reconciliation with the pleasure principle less likely. Competitive sport could be described as the absolute opposite of play, which is 'unproductive and useless, precisely because it rejects the repressive and exploitative features of labour and leisure, it is "merely playing" with the truth'. Not only is sport now accepted and integrated as one of the performing arts (alongside theatre, dance or cinema), but it is also seen as an art in its own right. Any comparison or identification is now permissible between the artist and the athlete, with the 'technical' moves seen in the 'beautiful game' – a dribble, a lob shot, a 'Panenka' – elevated to the status of major works of art. This strange substitution has been made possible by the hollowing or more exactly the ending of a certain historic autonomy of art. Similarly, acceptance of a possible 'end of art' has been made possible by the establishment of a rationalized socio-political system in which sport is the current 'utopian' aesthetic form. The classical aesthetic of art has been relegated as a 'thing of the past', to use Hegelian language, and replaced by a sporting aesthetic whose main components are violence done to bodies and the visualization of their brutal collisions amid the mass emotional clamour of a spectacle associated with stadiums.

This sporting aesthetic is essentially visual; seeing, visualizing, is the immediate sensory channel in sport, without resort to the other senses, let alone to rational thought; and this goes for athletes as well as spectators. The sporting aesthetic does not connect with the classical forms of visual art (painting, sculpture, architecture) or the unified forms of diversion society has adopted in recent years, the long tempo of a theatre play or movie or TV drama, or the even longer one of reading. The sporting aesthetic corresponds to a new and separate form: the ephemeral, the precarious associated with the brutal under the rule of a quite sketchy technique that can be seen in the tired moves of automated players, trained to repeat them ceaselessly, exhibited to the world's sport-habituated gaze through the different screens. We are thus witnessing, without the chance to refuse, the concoction of a globalized aesthetic of the sporting gesture as a technique rivalling art, and perhaps even a definitive substitution; a sporting aesthetic to which visualization is the best access route. The power of sport depends in fact on the power of glimpses of bodies in movement that it affords to the live or TV spectator. That is where the 'beauty' of sport has its source, in the way the athlete is transformed in the spectator's gaze into a heavily sexualized object. For everything in sporting body-language is an invitation to the intensive scrutiny of bodies whose essence is strongly tinged with sexuality: quasi-nudity, masochistic suffering, sometimes intimate body contact …

In counterpoint to his analysis of a universal aesthetic dimension in opposition to a Marxist aesthetic of Stalinist type, Herbert Marcuse admitted that beauty 'can be a quality of a regressive as well as progressive (social) totality. One can speak of the beauty of a fascist festival (Leni Riefenstahl has filmed it!)'. For to the philosopher, the sources of radical power in the idea of beauty 'are first in the erotic quality of the Beautiful, which persists through all changes in "judgment of taste".' Before being circumscribed by the analyses advanced by artists, philosophers and art theorists (Vitruvius, Alberti, Kant, Schiller, Hegel, Klee …), categories of harmony and utility, purposiveness without purpose and so on, beauty is characterized, according to Herbert Marcuse, by its erotic fluid, an inexhaustible spring that colours its surroundings.

As pertaining to the domain of Eros, the Beautiful represents the pleasure principle. Thus it rebels against the prevailing reality principle of domination. The work of art speaks the liberating language, invokes the liberating images of the subordination of death and destruction to the will to live. That is the emancipatory element in aesthetic affirmation.

The work of art participates in this liberation from the everyday because the everyday does not satisfy it. It does not duplicate reality, although it may lay claim to it and sometimes extract the best part of it. Nor does it reproduce it in some plastic form or other. For Marcuse, in other words,

the radical qualities of art, that is to say, its indictment of the established reality and its invocation of the beautiful image [schöner Schein] of liberation are grounded precisely in the dimensions where art transcends its social determination and emancipates itself from the given universe of discourse and behaviour while preserving its overwhelming presence. Thereby art creates the realm in which the subversion of experience proper to art becomes possible: the world formed by art is recognized as a reality which is suppressed and distorted in the given reality.

Unlike the art that makes sublimation possible by representing, for Adorno and Horkheimer,

fulfillment in its brokenness. The culture industry does not sublimate: it suppresses. By constantly exhibiting the object of desire, the breasts beneath the sweater, the naked torso of the sporting hero, it merely goads the unsublimated anticipation of pleasure, which through the habit of denial has long since been mutilated as masochism … The mechanical reproduction of beauty – which, admittedly, is made only more inescapable by the reactionary culture zealots with their methodical idolization of individuality – no longer leaves any room for the unconscious idolatry with which the experience of beauty has always been linked.

Unlike art, then, sport does not make possible any sort of non-repressive sublimation, either for the athletes or the spectators. The instincts that were sublimated by art are totally repressed by sport, which reduces play to the 'lure of the record' (Adorno). In other words, sublimation of the body is a principal characteristic of sport, but it becomes a repressive sublimation because, specifically, the athlete's body is subjected to productivity, to performance, to comprehensive rationalization. Moreover, sport embodies a tendency for this repressive sublimation to swing back towards repressive desublimation as its indispensable counterpart. Work and leisure are profoundly interwoven, and in sport – which is both work and leisure – they comprise together the prodigious, sovereign form of current mass culture. In its new space-time dimension, with the stadium doubling as the venue for the practice of sport and as televisual frame, sport has definitively replaced art because it has appropriated the sublimation component still present in play. It has transformed art – which is play, imaginative leap, take-off into dreamscape, free instinct – into a rational, functional performance technology.

What Léo Lagrange was already calling *le sport-spectacle* – 'show-sport' – in 1936, more specifically competitive sport, is today an overwhelming presence in the world and an increasingly oppressive one. Everyday life is effectively saturated by the omnipresence of sport which adheres to its smallest nooks and crannies. The endless flow of sporting imagery has invaded the private as well as the public sphere, making sport the most indestructible link between them, if not the only possible link. You could say that it is impossible for sport to be transformed into a work of art, still less a masterpiece, or to return to *play* (not play 'with' something: the play of life itself) because, far from questioning its own reality or the prevailing one, sport refracts them through the grille of its own repetitive structure. You could also say that sport modifies the world, but always in the direction of aesthetic impoverishment, of a realist duplication of the world in all its impoverished functionality. While sport as represented in photography, cinema, television or any other mediating mode gives only a trivial, fleeting picture of the reality (the goalkeeper's horrified face, the supporters lifting their arms in unison, the marathon runner's rictus of pain), art on the contrary sublimates the reality whose 'immediate content is stylized, the "data" are reshaped and reordered in accordance with the demands of the art form.' Marcuse writes:

It is precisely this Lebensweld which is transcended by the protagonists – as Shakespeare's and Racine's princes transcend the
courtly world of absolutism, as Stendhal's burghers transcend the
bourgeois world, and Brecht's poor that of the proletariat. This
transcendence occurs in the collision with their Lebensweld,
through events which appear in the context of particular social
conditions while simultaneously revealing forces not attributable
to these specific conditions.

True art, therefore, does not depend on reflecting raw reality. The work of art is, on the contrary, a process of transforming the real. So much so that even representations of sport considered 'artistic' in photography, cinema, the many exhibitions making use of sports objects (the football itself is a fetish-object) and sport as an artistic activity, merely serve to underline its crass physicality and assert its banal presence. Sport can only assert its presence, it can never shake or question that presence. Its 'content' does not allow it to become a wholesale component of art. The work of art, Marcuse writes, 'is beautiful to the degree to which it opposes its own order to that of reality – its non-repressive order where even the curse is still spoken in the name of Eros'.

Sport – football, rugby, athletics – is subject by definition to the requirements of repressive sublimation through bodily release, the violent redirection of libidinal energies, the gross clash of pha-lanxes of massive bodies being trampled, kicked, punched, elbowed in a welter of collisions, collapsed scrums and high tackles, brutal verging on bestial. The 'eroticization' of sport, linked to performance regarded as a measure of perfection, is accomplished in the struggle between athletes hungry for supremacy and keen to fight it out on field or track. In other words, while a specific 'eroticism' and 'aes-thetic' that gush out of sport are associated here, they correspond to performance, violence, struggle and the most trivial bodily release. Sport thus shares in a *declining aesthetic*: extreme value placed on confrontation or clash, exhibition of bodily sufferings, over-valued gregarious body language, but technique often reduced to the com-pulsive repetition of moves (the famous 'automatisms') and gestures of psychological preparation (ritual religious signs, ostentatious warming-up postures, etc.).

On a more spatial level, the development of sport is linked to architectural monumentalism and technologization plus the recurrent geometrization of nature, making for an abstract universe. Repressive desublimation is manifested not only on the sexual level, in the form of a *reified eroticization* of bodies (instant gratification of sexual impulses, intensification of libido) and repression of the ability to reject the world, but also and above all in sport as the reified projection of that eroticization. Adorno noted that 'technicization' had made our gestures (and by the same token, the people making them) 'rigid and stale'. It deprives gestures of all hesitation, circumspection and 'refinement', bending them to the 'intransigent demands', as it were without history, that are made by 'things'. The possibility of an emancipatory aesthetic, on the other hand, must necessarily refer back to the 'vision' of a non-repressive order in which 'the subjective and objective world, man and nature, are harmonized'. The non-repressive order, Marcuse concludes, is essentially an order of 'abundance'. That is certainly not a description of sport as we see it here.

15. SEXUALITY AND SPORT

One of the more visible features of competitive sport has been the development of latent homosexual comportments among players in the same team, based on sadomasochistic collusion (aggressiveness and 'pleasure' in pain) or group narcissism ('We are the champions!'). The latent homosexuality in social groups brought to light by Freud – notably in what he called 'artificial groups', the Church and the Army in particular – is especially apparent when the social groups are not of mixed gender. Without wishing to force an analogy or comparison, one could say that that was true of the Nazi bands in Germany and is true of almost all teams in collective sport, football and rugby in particular. Vladimir Jankélévich forcefully reminds us:

> Spartan austerity, Greek nudity, gymnosophy were the classic nineteenth-century forms of German delirium. The Hitlerian athlete of the twentieth century is dressed, armed, girded, booted, helmeted, caparisoned, but the homosexual inclination is more pronounced than ever. Everything shows it: the display of brute strength and reverence for muscle, gladiators' pectorals twitching behind shining cross-belts, the madness of uniforms that once hypnotized a conquered France as it was fascinated by the handsome blond barbarians: France on her knees, seduced, subjugated, yielding miserably to delicious violation by her tall long-skulled ravisher: for the defeat had been caused by voluptuous consent to defeat and a feeble yielding to the lordly race.

The calendar of the stripped-down 'gods of the stadium', the French national rugby team, has been a monstrous illustration of all this for years now: a blend of sport and pornography ('sporn' for short) displayed in shameless homo-Graeco-gigolo style with the exhibition of gorgeous, scantily clad, often fair-haired hunks with the perfect physiques of Greek statues, typically lounging in languid semi-pornographic poses, a glimpse of something trying to thrust through the revealing slot in the bulging boxer shorts, skin oiled or moisturized or glistening under shower jets, two to a cubicle ... What is deployed is the entire spectrum of fantasized neo-fascist carnality: the enormity, the disproportion of monumental bodies built piece by piece, muscles bulging under the skin to form unwieldy lumps of flesh, humps, protuberances, gibbosities, swellings, so many ridiculous excrescences. The skin is glossy, smooth, scrubbed, often oiled and apparently depilated, and sometimes heavily decorated with truckers' tattoos. Men strike warrior poses with armour (knee pads, shin guards, bandana, scrum cap); the eyes are hard, tense, but the faces a little sleepy and lascivious, sometimes with a hint of sly seductiveness ...

According to Adorno and Horkheimer, contemporary mass society, of which sport constitutes the archetype, is regressing towards infantile polymorphous perversity. Society has built an impregnable genital façade whose completion is expressed, in football for example, by the presence of the players' wives and girlfriends in the stands as an autonomous and differentiated sexual group. The WAGs form their own bloc, speak with one voice, celebrate goals together and weep and console each other in moments of defeat. After the game, the tired warriors have the right to relax in the arms of their concubines ... it is an amalgam of infantile regression and true-blue machismo.

In sport, the erotic ideal is taken back to a pregenital stage mainly through its anal-sadistic component whose active element is deployed, according to Freud, in the instinct or wish to dominate, itself linked to the musculature. To grasp the pregenital character of the sporting 'personality' it suffices to observe the behaviour of team players after a goal, a try or a win: jumping on each other, embracing in a group hug, rolling on the ground in a heap, doing dance routines or whacking themselves on the buttocks, generally celebrating like little kids. In rugby, the scrum is the main setting for this anal eroticism, deflected from all pleasure, essentially massified and focused on the other team, the adversary: a scene of engagement, penetration, thrust, but desexualized, like another way to what Adorno called the 'desexualization of sex itself'. Then, the musculature of each player contributes to the collective effort via its grip on the bodies of others, the grunting face-to-face collision of the two mountains of muscle, that way of crouching on all fours that typifies olfactory regression. The bipolar presence of active and passive elements is especially obvious during football or rugby tournaments. In football, for example, the character of repressed homosexuality is present before the game in the way it is mounted, and compounded by an infantilizing but nonchalant walk from the changing rooms to the pitch by the players of both teams, each hand in hand with a child. The casual innocence of this ritual or exhibition at the beginning of every big match completes to perfection the apparatus of regressive infantilism eagerly awaited by the enthusiastic crowd.

As something that exacerbates male sexual tension, sport accentuates this regression into infantile, archaic and narcissistic stages of development. The group of players is a small army in marching order, emotionally swayed by the equivocal pleasure leading it out from intimate and private gathering places (changing rooms, showers, training grounds), and perhaps all the way to the public setting of a victory parade (Circus Maximus, Champs-Élysées, Piccadilly). Lifted into the firmament of media stardom, the group of male sportsmen constitutes a sort of warrior pack whose – sometimes conflictual – unity is cemented with the 'desexualized, homosexual and sublimated love for other men which is born out of common labour': a labour which here, in fact, may be merging with sport.

This situation can be compared with that of a distinctive collectivity from the past. In the fascist group (Adorno and Horkheimer thought), with its teams and training camps, everyone from their earliest youth is a prisoner in segregated detention, which favours the development of homosexuality. The sports domain – whose hermetic character is ensured by the enclosed spaces of the stadium and training centres – also boosts the development of a collective atmosphere strongly coloured with repressed homosexuality and an endogamous, gregarious sexuality, with like seeking like in the narcissistic intoxication and megalomaniac enjoyment of 'victory'. The sports team as a collective structure, militarized with commando discipline (an army course was organized for the French rugby team in preparation for the 2007 World Cup), represents a resurgence of the spirit of the horde or hunting pack whose objective is dominance, predation, humiliation. In that sense, football or rugby teams form an archaic male structure whose bestiality and cult of physical violence resemble in their instinctive and ideological character those of other hordes animated by the absence of scruples, the justification of brutal force and the destruction of the competitor, adversary or 'enemy'. For Adorno and Horkheimer, the reappearance of the 'horde' in the organization of the Hitler youth was not a return to old-fashioned barbarism, but the triumph of 'repressive equality'. Their analysis enables us here to appreciate sport as a matrix of regression on the instinctual level, as finally no more nor less than a structure for the fascization of the masses, the grouping into a dense mass of numberless individuals reduced to the level of simple supporters.

16. THE RELIGION OF SPORT

In this happy sporting globalization, delivering an image of the world embellished by being a sporting one, what is the social status of the athlete? Can he or she be seen as a free worker, an individual possessing no saleable asset other than their labour power, that is, their body? Marx told us long ago that labour power was realized externally; that it was asserted and made apparent through labour which involved a certain expenditure of the worker's 'muscle, nerve and brain', something meriting compensation. There is an immediately obvious analogy with modern competitive sport, whose athletes are bought and sold as freely available labour power on the vast, planetary performances and records market. Sporting labour power is thus directly dependent on the social relation between sellers and buyers. If it is not sold and bought it doesn't exist, there's nothing there.

This particular labour power has a variable scale of value, tending to acquire greater value and even to be exchanged against other high values, or on the contrary to diminish as degraded or declining exchange value, when the athlete is no longer close enough to the top of the international competitive hierarchy. Apart from that, the development of the sporting labour power on which competition is based also includes the fabrication of surplus value, that 'great secret of modern society' (and of capitalism itself). The athlete for his part performs labour of a specific type – which for some individuals can be very highly rewarded – creating surplus labour (the difference between the market value of his labour and what he is paid for it) from which a sometimes substantial surplus value can be extracted. While most ordinary labour is measured in terms of the quantity of objects produced or the palpable results of a service performed, the athlete's labour has to be measured by the records or performances achieved; their constant 'advances' are the indices of qualitative and quantitative difference. As the very top workers in their fields, sportsmen and women are recompensed in part with planetary visibility.

During the rise of capitalist society, sport in its own autonomous development was at first aligned with classical wage labour and the structural chain that goes with it: competition, productivity, measurement and records (or performances). As it became more autonomous, sport 'emancipated' itself from the traditional labour form to emerge as total labour, overarching the classical typology of labour. It has ceased to be a different form of traditional labour – a parallel form, 'freer' by definition than the average – and become the modern form taken by labour under the capitalism that prevails at the start of the third millennium.

- 'Sport is tied to industry because it represent(s) a reaction against industrial life.'
- 'Sport is an essential factor in the creation of the mass man.'
- 'In sport, as elsewhere, nothing gratuitous is allowed to exist; everything must be useful and must come up to technical expectations.'
- 'In sport the citizen of the technical society find(s) the same spirit, criteria, morality, actions, and objectives – in short, all technical laws and customs – which he encounters in office or factory.'

These notes by Jacques Ellul (lecture notes, *The Technological Society*) are spot on, even though he fails to round them off by pointing out the rise of sport as a new and renewed intrinsic form of labour, and no longer just its extension.

In any case, labour in the office, factory or fields is no longer considered these days as a prestigious value (or even one worth mentioning), let alone as an activity for improving the body. Since the rise of the leisure society in the early twentieth century, social recognition of the classic forms of labour has been increasingly displaced towards sport – sport seen as a different labour form, a metamorphosed form that has largely replaced traditional labour. The perpetual accumulation of performances and records, the principle of sporting productivity and the profitability associated with it, are the cornerstones of a sports culture which now dominates the standard imagery if not the whole imagination of individuals, and perhaps even everyday life itself. Every infinitesimal improvement in time or space plays a part in creating some sporting surplus value, endlessly increasing under the rule of perpetual improvement in records and performances. Sport has occupied everyday life completely and is restructuring it from the ground up, as labour did in the past, but with its own organization, and in its own specific image. Daily life, once perceived in relation to traditional labour with its negative connotations (graft, grief, work, drudgery) is now associated with sport whose traits seem altogether positive (health, beauty, upward social mobility). Sport, in other words, has been definitively written into everyday life and today even resembles everyday life. It is projected effortlessly as the new common religious value, a supreme value that consigns the classical religion of labour at a stroke to the oubliettes of memory. The everyday – the articulation of everyday time and space – is not just invaded but punctuated, its rhythms taken over, by sporting events and their local, national and international manifestations. Worldwide sport has been anointed as a planetary religion, as well as a substitute for traditional labour. From international to local (and vice versa), the huge contemporary power of sport is deployed through the infinite multiplication of sport and of its endlessly renewed image.

17. THE CRITIQUE OF
SPORT AS IT WAS

Much has changed since the 1970s, but a critical review of the arguments advanced by the critique of sport sketched out in that period of radical denunciation and militancy is still necessary. The present time is remarkable above all for the irresistible power with which sport has expanded across the planet, leading to its successful and nearly complete globalization. The first objective element damaging to critical positions on sport lies in the irresistible power of a mass phenomenon that has no equal today. Relentless pounding in the media pulverized most critical positions, their proponents literally excluded from mainstream discussions, polemics and debates on sport; if they are still allowed expression here and there, it's preferably out of the public eye and in verbally hostile conditions. The second fundamental element, which is connected to the first, is that what the critique of sport did manage to say has now been overtaken by reality itself. While it was commonplace, in the 1970s, to denounce great state institutions – the justice system, the army, education, but also exploitation of labour and labour itself – sport was not criticized with the same radical zeal. For example, the exploitation of factory labour (repetitive tasks, alienation, numbing of the mind) was a main theoretical and practical axis of determined and incisive criticism, with the long-term but stated objective of putting an end to work as a source of alienation. Yet the sporting institution slipped easily through the meshes of the critical net, and no part of its immense pyramidal organization (from local clubs to international bodies) had to suffer the sort of seismic shocks common in those heated years.

This helps to explain why sport as an institution today is in the vanguard of 'non-criticism'. Indeed, it is for that very reason that sport has wormed its way into the vanguard of everything. However, the fact is that criticism of society in general, and of sport in particular, has in recent years lost most of its radical content to offer a plodding, often complacent description of events in the world. Of course this retreat from criticism is not specific to sport, but is part of a much wider decline of social criticism directed among other things to the domains of art and culture, and to a number of institutions including the state itself. Perhaps harder to admit is that the critique of sport is no longer even capable of performing a critical function because it has failed to reproduce itself and is now congealed, solidified. But the primary cause of the collapse of militant criticism, theoretical and practical, is the weight of 'victories' won by sport, principally an alienating process of massification, the ideal of globalization through the spectacle of mass emotional excess boosted and transmitted by television, the integration and blending of sport with everyday life, and lastly the fall of the central taboo – against doping – which had constrained sport for so many years.

Two monster events precipitated this erasure of the critique of sport. The victory of the French team in the 1998 football World Cup, and to a lesser extent the 2006 final in which France lost to Italy, were both significant moments in the fading of the critical theory of sport, the collapse of its impact and of its militant campaigning. Under repeated attack from football (and lately rugby too) presented as a life model ('*la vie en bleu*'), raised to the level of new republican path, 'civic' as they now call it, and in view of the consensus in its favour in political, academic and intellectual circles, the critique of sport could have vanished more or less without trace. Of course, more than forty years after the events of May–June 1968 it is easy to see how the original freshness of the radical critique of sport was eclipsed. The analyses made at the time no longer apply, in any case, for example the attempt to bring to light the relation between sport and politics – something difficult to prove at that time, or to advance as an argument. Rejected or denied in the 1960s and 70s, the symbiotic link between sport and politics is now accepted, indeed actively cultivated. We may even be witnessing a still closer rapprochement between sport and politics, almost their organic fusion, when a number of former or recent sportsmen have become eminent government supporters or political aediles. Quite a few politicians swear by sport alone or practise politics with sport as their metaphor. The traditional political game, political projects and big political themes are shot through with sport in the sense that sport is this mode of social production and reproduction (everything is sport, everyone is sporting, sport is the most important thing there is), even and especially when its political character is being denied. 'I've heard two candidates suggesting a boycott of the Beijing Games,' Sarkozy was reported as saying:

> Boycott Beijing … but that isn't what sport is for. It's more important than anything. And why? Because it's one of the small joys. For myself, when I was young, in Royan, I used to slip out to watch the Tour de France at three o'clock in a bar called Le Plaisance. I'll never forget it. It's inside me for life. Sport's a cultural thing. If you don't have it, you won't catch on. (*Libération*, 14 April 2007).

So sport is really political through and through, and it's not just a state politics, or the sporting politics of every state; sport is the form politics takes in our societies today. Sport as metapolitics? One could even suggest that the only real party, globalized from the start in the sense of being an organic, 'living' representation of society, in its history, through its development and intrinsic dynamic, is the party of sport with its leaders, its members, its sympathizers and its rejects … facing the various traditional parties, not very different from one another, but still tolerated as a sort of makeweight.

18. THE ARRIVAL OF SPORT AS AN ACADEMIC DISCIPLINE

Since the attempted boycott of the football World Cup in Argentina in 1978, no political movement of comparable scope has arisen to challenge any aspect of sport. Unlike the critiques of other institutions, critical theory on sport has had very little concrete influence on the thinking of most intellectuals and academics, and even less on the course of things. Most intellectuals were not much interested in the first place, and finally opted to turn their guns against those who had dared to attempt radical criticism of competitive sport. Unable to discern in sport one of the great totalitarian systems of modern times, most intellectuals and academics rallied round it, very often adopting an openly populist posture ('The people are there, let's be there too!').

Even in a context of overall critical retreat and populist enthusiasm for anything that moves, the fact remains that no other globalized social phenomenon has been as exempt – if that's the word – from criticism. Should this attitude be understood as an omission, or as a new *trahison des clercs*, or again as a result of the extinction of intellectuals as an organic group capable of a dynamic analysis of the aspects of society with which sport is most connected? Just as some French universities have accepted as respectable the fraudulent discipline known as Staps (Science and technology of physical and sporting activities), it is to be noted that the majority of academics and intellectuals in the world have incorporated sport into their positive reference zones. With very few exceptions, they have flocked in serried ranks to give eager endorsement to sport and its links to such prized values and qualities as solidarity, integration, aesthetics

... A lot of academics are now among the most fervent supporters of the sporting cause. They are sport's fiercest champions, touting it as an instrument that could save society's soul. While the universities earned little prestige from their shabby capitulation over Staps, they have themselves become a zone of competition on all fronts: between universities now considered competitors, between research teams and colleagues, between students, and so on, all in a sporting register: be the best by crushing the rest. In just a few years, taking its cue from the sporting model, university has become the new school of mass training in 'winning at all costs'. Inflation of the sporting model in society has taken the form of a 'new education'. Sport did not enter the university as just another discipline, like philosophy or sociology, with its own history, its own specialized knowledge and its critical component. On the other hand it may have played a part in demolishing the universities, helped by the absence of any active criticism of its barbarism and the inability to see the transformation of its teachings into a vast curriculum vitae, literally that so aptly named 'race for life', now a competition within the university. Might universities too have bought into the essential parameters of sport: competition-output-measurement-record? Might they too have become competitive arenas, in the image of sport?

19. THE FUTURE OF THE CRITIQUE OF SPORT

The question of the future of the critique of sport, then, remains open in the early twenty-first century. It could be examined in these terms: critique is a singular posture that means confronting an object, sport in this instance, but in the middle of an immense scrum involving all the interested parties. It directs its goad towards its object, which then constitutes a target. Critique is not supercilious or detached from the real movement, whose product it is. The critique of sport is primarily a matter of contesting it theoretically and practically, mounting a determined and determining opposition to the powerful, durable structure of the 'sports-spectacle' and its colossal tentacular organization. The force of the words used gives no indication of how radical or subtle the critique may be; that resides in the posture of those who step forward to utter it at all important moments, like great sporting occasions, as well as opposing sport in general from a serious theoretical and practical viewpoint. The critique of sport lies at the heart of any examination of a project for society, in so far as sport now lies at the heart of society.

Some of the more backward critics still see the essential contradictions in sport as doping, violence and racism, regarded as regrettable, but extraneous, scourges. Our view is that the chief contradiction in sport lies between the irresistible globalizing drift whose reflection and project it is, and the former structures linked to its own history and diverse national roots. At the same time as sport is developing as a worldwide system and market, its earlier roots are keeping it in the framework of the nation-states which remain the hegemonic foundations on which it is still structurally seated. So the main contradiction arising out of sport is the discord or mismatch between the supranational structures sport has formed (IOC, UEFA, FIFA, etc.) and the national structures it has inherited, of which competition is both the arena and the driving force, with the result that while a record is the achievement of an individual national athlete, it is primarily a world-scale milestone. With sport, everything conspires to globalize it even when the bulk of its activities are still organized in national territories.

Max Horkheimer stated that the task of critical theory was to express what is not, as a rule, expressed. This task cries out to be pursued today through the critique of sport, not merely to describe one by one its more obviously indefensible characteristics (doping, racism, violence) but rather to show that the totalitarian-barbaric aspect of sport is its major feature, now built into contemporary world society, both in its base (economy, institutions) and in its superstructure (ideology, culture). The critical theory of sport is not just another sociological current or school of thought, complete with masters and disciples; still less is it a sect dining out on its 'critical' accomplishments. It is a mobile apparatus for action against the sporting institution. The critique of sport seeks to 'dynamite' all those notions on the function, role and value of sport that seem at best naive, at worst ecumenical or shamelessly gushing: education, beauty, humanism ... The critique of sport, like any true critique, has no positive side. Its sole claim to 'positivity' is its consistently, resolutely negative attitude to sport as it is, even to the extent of denying its own systematic negativity – criticism – by disappearing at the right moment.

Who belongs to this critical current? Does it even amount to a current, a movement, or is it just the huddle of a few individuals? Who can make use of it? Is there a project behind this critical stance? Individuals, always well-intentioned, sidle up from time to time to see what it's all about; they tiptoe or lumber closer to a more or less stable core; they make eyes at it, try to stroke its outlines, manage to grasp a couple of snippets of analysis and aspire to fit in. But these protocritics seldom stay in its field of action for long, hauled away as they are by formidable centrifugal forces: diverse institutional commitments, career plans, retreat into private life, above all the inability to sustain an analysis ... The protocritics of the critique of sport continue nevertheless to circle around that nucleus of individuals, quite restricted in number but theoretically unbeatable; a nucleus that is called upon now and then to recompose itself, in a perpetual dialectic of theoretical and practical struggle.

Contrary to what some of the dozy landlords and small farmers of criticism would like to think, a plan for the critique of sport, in the sense of a lasting critique with a timetable, cannot exist. The very idea of a plan for a critique of sport is nonsense. Those who were its most pertinent and incisive critics at a given moment could thus lose their legitimate place, if they prove no longer capable of producing an up-to-the-minute analysis of the development of sport in its real, current contradictions. Sport has at least the virtue of forcing a constant revision of analyses on anyone wishing to avoid endless repetition of what seems to have been established for ever. The critique of sport provides no job income. By losing all relation with the sport-object itself, these pseudo-critics of sport have actually engaged in a sort of intellectual divagation, a hallucinatory pursuit of thought for thought's sake. 'No theory,' Adorno reminds us in *Prisms*, 'not even the true one, is secure from perversion into madness once its spontaneous relation to the object has been externalized'.

Like a projectile hurtling into its target, the critical theory of sport had succeeded in hitting the monolithic bloc of the sporting institution, leaving some visible dents. But the institution knew better than to defend itself. It reacted by rapidly plugging the superficial holes and completing its deployment across the whole planet; it structured itself in a double movement from global to local, from summit to base, spreading an efficient sporting ideology. This ideology entered all the more easily into minds already numbed with a decadent modernity, having already infected the whole of society with its irrepressible power. The mass sports-spectacle has received support in recent years from numerous intellectuals of left and right in search of media recognition; it has been followed and adulated by a host of journalists eager to stay as close as possible to a reality that fascinates them; as for the young, they have lapped it up greedily. Sport is thus enjoying, unarguably, a new aura of good publicity, having itself become the new medium projecting a general consensus on its great capacity to embellish the world. Sport is out to re-enchant life and, as we put it earlier, to become the grandiose project of a projectless society.

Naturally, critical sport theory, like any theory meant to be critical, needs constant updating to accommodate the changing, shifting reality, the permanent mutation of its raison d'être – the thing it depends on, analyses and attacks. It also goes without saying that there can be no sport criticism movement without the theory to support it. That may be one of the reasons for the virtual absence these days of an efficacious theoretical critique associated with effective militant practice. This decline is not apparent from the number of its adherents, which has never been very large, but from its loss of grip on reality and its material and intellectual incapacity to resist the reality of sport in appropriate ways. These would include the presence of an organ embodying original opposition, able to confirm the rigour and authority of the critique at the right moment. That supportive organ, for some of the time between its first appearance in April 1975 and its self-dissolution in 1997, was the journal *Quel corps?* which stood up magnificently to the whole spectrum of pro-sport forces (ranging from extreme right to extreme left, via the liberal right and the French Communist Party). *Quel corps?* had certainly reached the end of its useful life by the time it was wound up. It should be noted however that being an 'effective support' in this context involved an indissociable unity of effective form with effective content; the material projection of an anti-sport content made the journal, just as the journal constituted authoritative support for that content.

The question that probably most bothers the more radical despisers of sport today is whether the reality of sport is still comparable with that of the 1960s and 70s, or whether it has changed fundamentally. Might it not have been shaken to the core by, among other things, the rapid, powerful globalization of recent years? To hasten straight to the point, my conviction, based on research rather than simple opinion, is that society's space and time are now shot through with sport and perhaps already dependent on it through several interlinked phenomena, including its irresistible expansion under the dominance of football alone, enveloping the planet and worming its way into every dwelling, every individual, through the televising of sporting competitions; the incorporation or assimilation into the enterprise of all its bad aspects and losses of direction, all the excesses which now lie at the heart of sporting spectacle, the cement of that spectacle if not the spectacle as such. The world's time and space are hinged together to make the world future of sport into the sports future of the world.

What this means is that – apart from money, of course – it is doping and violence that have become the central, determinant, living elements of sport-spectacle, not just essential but fundamental and definitive. They are no longer the marginal, peripheral or external phenomena they seemed in the 1960s and 70s; the new triptych of money-violence-doping is in the middle of sport, part of its common matrix, in the final analysis the thing that enables it to go on developing, as it were proliferating; that enables it literally to exist. Without generalized doping in cycle racing, to take a widely-known example (which can however be extended to all the sporting disciplines), that sport would no longer exist and the sports-spectacle in general would have lowered the curtain and shut up shop years ago.

Fundamentally, then, sport is no longer a phenomenon like others, detached from a general context, but rather the conjunction of all the most detestable phenomena to be found in society, among them violence (not really under control), doping (under perfect control) and commercial rapacity (money) in all of which it is saturated to the core. Neither this radical transformation of scale in sport, nor that of the whole space-time continuum that contains it (of which it is one of the agents, and which has upset the very structure of its spectacle with its power to contaminate everyone alive), has been analysed in all its socio-political depth. A critique of sport adjusted to everyday normality over the years has failed to register today's *incorporation* of violence and doping, after the earlier acceptance of money, by the sports-spectacle as an integral part of its structure. This deficiency in the critique of sport was one of the causes of its decline. In fact it may have been fatal to that earlier critique, which in any case had become far too smug, far too convinced of its own critical righteousness, persuaded that it had furnished the weapons of the critique of sport once and for all, that it had produced the definitive theory in the form of the *thèses*, now congealed, but forgetting to cast a critical eye over the weapons themselves. The rusted guns are still there, but they don't fire any more … *The theory has gone cold*. One might say that the overwhelming power of sport as a vector of socio-political and ideological propagation in our societies put external stress on the critique, while internally there developed a chronic failure of analysis on the part of sport's most resolute adversaries. The combination ended by *corroding* the critique, then *decomposing* it, and finally *dissolving* it.

In the pestilential environment oozing out of sport, the question arises: what can critical theory come up with today against sport now it has become the visible face of every society? The only possible critical response is a firm assertion: *there should be no sport.*

APPENDIX I
TWENTY THESES ON SPORT

I THE BIRTH OF MODERN CAPITALIST SPORT

1. While it is true that humanity has always engaged in physical exercise for playful, competitive, utilitarian or military purposes – collective games, hunting, ritual physical exercises etc. – it is false to claim that sport is 'as old as the hills' or 'part of the heritage of humanity'. *Such mystical conceptions present sport ahistorically, as a transcendent entity, over and above historical periods and modes of production.*

2. Sport as an *institution* is the product of a historical turning point. Sport appeared in England, the birthplace of the capitalist mode of production, at the beginning of the modern industrial epoch. From the start, sport was not a homogenous institution but a *class practice*. Sport meant different things for different social classes. While for the bourgeoisie sport was conceived as a leisure pursuit and a form of distraction, the proletariat experienced the need for sport as a means of physical recuperation. This explains why the workers' movement has since its inception adopted the demand for the right to sport along with the right to work, and has fought for this demand within the struggle for the reduction of working hours.

3. Britain exported her main forms of sporting practices along with her commodities and gunboats, to India, Southern Africa, etc. *The birth of world sport parallels the consolidation of imperialism.* The great international sports federations were set up at the turn of the

century around the time of the First World War, at the same time as the other great supranational organizations such as the League of Nations. Today the international authorities of world sport are completely integrated into the mechanisms of imperialism.

4. Sport is a consequence of the level of development of the productive forces under capitalism. It is a product of the reduction of working hours, of urbanization and the modernization of the means of transport. Sport *itself* turns the body into an instrument which it helps to integrate into the complex system of productive forces. Such a relative development of the productive forces is in *stark contrast to the chronic under-development of physical potential* in the countries dominated by imperialism, reflected in malnutrition, deformities and so on.

5. This development of physical potential through sport has taken place in the context of bourgeois production relations. As a class institution, sport reproduces these production relations in an ideological form. In this respect sport has become *state monopoly sport,* totally controlled by the centralized state apparatus. This is why any perspective of reform is illusory. Sport must be smashed, like the state machine.

6. *The institution of sport is geared into the mechanisms of the capitalist system.* Sports clubs operate like firms competing on the sports market. The capitalists of sport appropriate players and athletes who thus become their wage laborers. Within the clubs, the class struggle takes on the specific form of a struggle between the suppliers of capital and the suppliers of performances. The relations between the managements and sportsmen are *wage relations*, with all that this implies: exploitation of the capacity to produce performances, sports trade unionism etc.

7. The competitive sportsman is *a new type of worker* who sells his labour power – that is to say his ability to produce a spectacle that draws the crowds – to an employer. The exchange value of his labor power, governed by the law of supply and demand on the market, is determined by the labour time socially necessary for its production. Amateurism ceased to exist a long time ago. All top-level sportsmen

are professional performers in the muscle show. They are also very often advertising 'sandwich-board' men.

8. The sports system is thus an integral part of the capitalist mode of production, constituting a specific sector within the capitalist division of labour. Economic trusts, banks and monopolies have taken over the financial side of sporting activity, which has become a prized source of capitalist profits. Competition for these profits is spurred on by the profits of competition. Hence the number of sports competitions is stepped up in order to speed up the circulation of sports capital and the production of surplus value.

9. Mass spectator sport is a vast capitalist enterprise within the entertainments industry – hence part of the tertiary sector. The commercialization of sport operates on four principal levels:

- the establishment of a sports products, goods and services industry – winter sports, tourism, the equipment market etc.
- the development of spectator sport as a base for advertising
- the tapping of citizens' (and particularly workers') resources to swell the coffers of the stadiums
- likewise, for the sports betting industry – racing, the pools etc.

The sports system is thus an integral part of a massive monetary circulation network, which means that any hope of 'cleaning up sport' financially speaking is an illusion.

10. The numerous and frequent scandals affecting the sports system – fraud, tax evasion, extortion, illegal transfers, bankruptcies and various shady schemes – are a specific reflection of the crisis of state monopoly capitalism and its disintegration through inflation, unemployment etc. This crisis will inevitably give rise to struggles on the part of the practitioners and consumers of sport, in which we will have to intervene.

11. International economic competition between imperialist and bureaucratic state focuses around the struggle over who will organize major international sports meetings such as the Olympics. Such events require considerable capital investments and contribute to

regional or national economic development, through the opening up of markets, the provision of facilities etc. *The growing scale of the Olympics reflects the pressure of the economic, political, diplomatic and military combines which are set up to profit from them.*

THE IDEOLOGICAL FUNCTIONS OF SPORT

1. *Sport has the function of justifying the established order.* Sport is a *positivist system* and as such always plays an integrating and never an oppositional role. This justificatory function flows from sport's typically optimistic ideology of indefinite, linear progress. Progress can only lead to *improvement*, and hence any system which brings it about must be intrinsically good. Whether in the East or in the West, sport everywhere aims to get the masses to *acclaim* the established socio-political system as a whole. Sport thus functions as a *justification* of the joys of the 'American way of life' or the 'socialist system'.

2. *Sport is a stabilizing factor for the existing system.* By conning people into identifying with the champions, sport has a depoliticizing effect. The champions are the positive heroes of the system: those who by their own efforts and labours have succeeded in climbing the rungs of the social ladder. They justify and reinforce the social hierarchy. By holding out this perspective of salvation via a parallel hierarchy, sport sows illusions in the possibility of social advancement:

- by camouflaging the class struggle, sport operates in every social formation in the world as a new type of opiate of the people. Social conflicts and the class struggle are acted out metaphorically in individual or collective muscular contests (cf. the ideology of sportsmanship);
- by the rationalization of the general myths of bourgeois society:
  - economic competition is presented metaphysically as an eternal given, whose playful representation is sport;
  - the hierarchy of sport which is maintained by the classification of physical performances assists the perpetuation of the hierarchic structure of capitalist production relations;
  - social inequalities are reproduced in exaggerated form

within sport, but are masked by the pretense of equality between competitors – everyone starts off under the same conditions;

- by stabilizing itself as an ideological bloc, distilling the ideology of its own apparatus– hierarchy, selection, training, competition, bureaucracy, formalism, etc. These ideological values are embodied in the ritualistic practices of protocol, ceremonial etc. which serve to maintain the consistency and unity of the institution of sport.

3. *Sport is a practical application of the ideology of 'peaceful coexistence between states with different social systems'.* This status quo is strengthened by the integration of sports organizations into the institutions of imperialism – The World Health Organization, the International Trade Union Bureau, UN, UNESCO etc. The Olympic ideology of the truce, of brotherhood and peace is an application of the notion of peaceful coexistence within sport. For a period of a month the struggles of oppressed classes and nations is supposed to come to a halt while they gaze at the 'gods of the stadium'. This ideology is constantly being contradicted by the reality of international conflicts. Thus the history of the Olympics has always been punctuated by the sound of gun-boats and struggles. In 1956 there was the Franco-British Suez expedition against Nasser's Egypt and the bloody repression of the Hungarian workers' councils by Khruschev's tanks. In 1968 the military junta of fascist Diaz Ordaz shot down several hundred revolutionary students in the Square of the Three Cultures, Mexico City. And then in Munich in 1972 the Games were held to a background of US imperialism bombing North Vietnam with napalm and anti-personnel bombs. Here we have the reality behind the 'Olympic peace', the so-called oasis of brotherhood which is really nothing but class collaboration between oppressors and oppressed.

4. *Sport is a way of preparing labour-power for capitalist industrial labour:*

- instilling into people, early in life, the principle of maximum output and the productivity of the organism;
- adapting the body to the principles of mechanized labour. Sport employs the same techniques in this respect as industry – the

division of labour, the encouragement of automatic reflexes, the formalization of all movements etc. Sport 'Taylorizes' the body and inculcates a moral code based on effort and labour, thereby contributing to the perpetuation of the exploitation of the working class;

• appearing as politically neutral, sport encourages class collaboration by illustrating the possibility of a reasonable dialogue between the participants (the 'two sides of industry'), under the supervision of an impartial referee (the state).

5. *Sport is a powerful factor of sexual repression.* In sport, the prevailing form of relation between individuals and their own bodies is a sadomasochistic one: pleasure in painful effort – 'The more it hurts, the more it's doing you good.' Sport combats eroticism by de-sexing the muscular and sensory apparatus. Specifically sexual pleasure is replaced with pleasure in painful movement. Sport operates as an antidote to sexual desire by channelling it into sporting effort. This explains the efforts of educationalists to get adolescents to practice sport, thus combatting masturbation and what are judged to be 'premature' sexual relations. The repressive and unhealthy homosexual atmosphere – the showers, changing rooms, 'virile' friendships etc. pervading sport (as in the army) – is the reflection of the permanent struggle to impose a well-regulated, genital sexuality through sport, capable of adapting to bourgeois monogamy.

6. Sport is a means of militarizing and regimenting youth.

• Hitler, Mussolini, Franco, Pétain and de Gaulle all used sport to regiment youth in their efforts to put out the flame of proletarian revolution. Sport serves this purpose by developing a *standardized image of the body,* regulating the way the adolescent relates to his or her own body and seeking to establish the ideology of the body as a sort of automated machine. As a 'character school', sport creates authoritarian, aggressive, narcissistic and obedient character types, preparing young people for integration into society and training them to operate as alienated machines on the capitalist market.

• Sport contributes to the militarization of youth with the aim of reinforcing the nation's military potential and preparing for imperialist war. It is worth noting that sport is held in high regard in the army and that the pioneers of physical and sports education were soldiers – Amoros, Baden-Powell, Hebert et al.

7. *The sports spectacle reinforces the commodity spectacle, by presenting, as a spectacle, human commodities.*

- The spectacle of sport magnetizes enormous crowds – up to a million 'live' and up to a billion via television. As the biggest mass spectacle, sport operates as a sort of catharsis machine, an apparatus for transforming aggressive drives. Instead of expressing them-selves in the class struggle, these drives are absorbed, diverted and neutralized in the sporting spectacle. Sport regulates and socializes aggression by providing permitted models of violence. Violence is thus codified, enabling all forms of direct action to be outlawed (put the shot instead of throwing bricks). So sport channels the energies of the masses in the direction of the established order.
- The spectacle of sport treats the masses as morons. Most of the mass media are saturated with trivial stories and futile sporting incidents (John Terry's sex life, Tim Henman's hamstring, etc.). The purpose of these meaningless dramas is to fill the masses' minds with trivia to prevent them thinking about political struggle.
- The spectacle of sport operates in such a way as to reduce the crowds, who provide it with 'cheering machines', to an undifferentiated mass in the stadiums, and in this respect it contributes to a process of emotional brutalization, reflected in march pasts, the profusion of flags, medal ceremonies, national anthems, salutes, etc. The surrounding of sports events with ostentatiously displayed security forces has the purpose of getting people used to their presence. The law and order of sport depends on maintaining law and order in general, and *vice versa*.

8. Within the totality of bourgeois superstructures sport has a special place at the intersection of three specific elements:

- the everyday institutionalization of the body
- the education system
- the spectacle of sport and the mass media

This accounts for the complexity and contradictory character of the institution of sport. In this respect, as in others, sport is affected by class contradictions and plays an important role in the class struggle.

9. Women are enslaved by the patriarchal structure of capitalist society. As a vector of ruling class ideology, sport reproduces this slavery and provides it with a justification in terms of the 'naturalness' of the individual. Sport aims to get women to be content with their subservient function:

- it institutionalizes sex differences – certain events do not exist for women – weightlifting, boxing, pole vault, etc;
- it structures women's bodies by systematizing specifically feminine myths into various sporting activities:
  - swimming, water ballet: the woman as siren or water nymph;
  - gymnastics, sprinting, high jump – all indicative of feline suppleness;
  - skating, ice dancing: grace and visual beauty;
  - shot put, throwing the hammer. cycling, etc. – the serious, active, hard-working woman – the homely creature.

The fact that women are tending to practise sports hitherto restricted to men (which are incidentally the most popular sports – football. rugby and so on) does not open up any perspective for their liberation, in that it identifies liberation with the emulation of men and hence perpetuates the patriarchal system. This is a sort of half-measure, leading via an apparently different form of alienation back to the same. It underlines the conception that discrimination is justified by natural difference and thus operates within the logic of the regime. The only true possibility of liberation is offered by the advent of communism.

These theses do not claim to be exhaustive. Their aim is to provide the basis for discussion, preliminary to the setting up of a bigger and more internationally based anti-Olympic committee than the one which emerged at the time of the Munich Olympics.

APPENDIX II
STOP BUILDING STADIUMS
IN EUROPE NOW!

OPEN LETTER TO *LIBÉRATION*, 21 MAY 2010

From Gérard Briche, France (philosopher), Eduarda Dionisio, Portugal (writer), Jean-Pierre Garnier, France (sociologist), Claude Javeau, Belgium (sociologist), Antonin Kosik, Czech Republic (philosopher), Véronique Nahum-Grappe, France (anthropologist), Marc Perelman, France (architect), Richard Sennett, USA (sociologist), Patrick Vassort, France (sociologist):

Are some of the countries now sunk in permanent and structural economic crisis, Portugal and Greece for example, going to lead the way? We refer not to their dissident posture over the threat to their own economies posed by risky domestic management and the context of global monetary speculation, but to the original political initiative by the former Portuguese Economy Minister Augusto Mateus, calling for the demolition of the stadiums built for Euro 2004. This proposal throws a powerful spotlight on the astonishing extravagance of public expenditure on sport and on football, especially at a time when Europe is undergoing a devastating crisis. The cost of building stadiums, then their permanent upkeep and the general maintenance of sites which most of the time are not in use, amounts to colossal financial losses that increasingly tear gaping holes in state budgets. While demolishing these stadiums is unlikely to stem the continuous money haemorrhage to any large extent, such a decision would at least help protect countries hosting major sporting events from the terrible consequences of sinking ever deeper into the financial abyss. The financial state of eighteen of the twenty British Premier League football clubs, for example, is perplexing to put it mildly, for their aggregate debt now amounts to some four billion euros. Before being relegated to the Football League Champtionship, Portsmouth United declared itself bankrupt and went into administration.

It is also worth noting that Canada only finished paying the bill for the 1976 Montreal Olympic Games in 2006; that the city of Grenoble took twenty-five years to settle its bill for the 1968 Winter Olympics; that the 2004 Athens Olympic Games cost the Greek taxpayer nine billion euros, 5 per cent of Greece's annual GDP, and also left the country with a heap of unused sporting installations; and that according to the BBC, the predicted cost of the 2012 London Olympics has already quadrupled from the original estimate. There are many less spectacular examples, all showing not only that sport is not a generator of income (the fallout from tourism is another great illusion), but that it is an endless cause of expenditure, like the leaky jar the Danaids have to spend eternity trying to fill, the epitome of useless investment. In sport, really, the more money you spend the more you need, stadiums being the bottomless money pits of an immense mess. For the next football World Cup, to be held in South Africa between 11 June and 11 July 2010, the five new stadiums and the five refurbished ones will cost a billion euros, with the total overall expenditure estimated at 7 billion − 30 per cent more than the original projected cost − against income of only 3.7 billion. Apart from all that, a Bank of America/Merrill Lynch study has concluded that between 1954 and 2006, the countries hosting competitions had achieved economic growth below their normal levels, not counting the working hours lost during transmission of the games!

On 28 May, the decision will be taken on which country (Turkey, Italy or France) is to host Euro 2016, the UEFA European Football Cup [Tr. note: France was chosen]. If France is chosen, it has yet to be established that the 1.74 billion euros earmarked for the construction or renovation of the twelve stadiums selected will be sufficient. What does all this mad new spending signify in France, and in a Europe teetering on the edge of recession, threatened with declining national economies and a declining EU? Of what genuine use is the stadium, in the present day, during this crisis threatening national economies with bankruptcy? For it is presented to us as a 'living space', a 'meeting space', a place for families to enjoy themselves; it represents, in the view of Jacques Herzog (one of the two architects of the 'Bird's Nest' Olympic stadium in Beijing), a 'democratic space', while Philippe Séguin once called it a place of 'general interest' for France.

It is well known that the stadium is not an enclosure cut off from its socio-political context, a neutral space, a simple tool, a mere arena for sporting competitions. The stadium is something quite other than an effective architectural frame. The stadium, everywhere in Europe, is an incubator of the worst sorts of violence, a place where the most repellent conducts flourish, whatever may be said by the many politicians, pseudo-sociologists and other phoney specialists always quick to minimize its frightful reality: xenophobia, anti-Semitism, racism, massive concentrations of every sort of stupidity, every sort of violence ...

This reality is not the work of a few dozen crazed hooligans, but of thousands of individuals gathered like assault troops and prone to an unleashing of instinctive savagery. So true is this that any mention of stadiums these days immediately reminds one of the repressive measures that have been taken as a direct consequence of the reprehensible acts so often committed inside or around them. The British Public Order Act of 1986 thus bans from the stadiums violent individuals known to the police; the later Football Offences Act (1991) makes racist or insulting chants, throwing missiles at players or invading the pitch imprisonable offences. In France, the proposed Hortefeux law will authorize temporary travel bans on football supporters; CCTV surveillance is widespread in and around most stadiums; a national database listing individuals banned from stadiums is generally available, while computerized tracking of spectators is being developed; not to mention telephone tapping, the shadowing of suspects and infiltration of gangs by undercover police, with (again in Britain) 'spotters', specialists trained to identify the features of individuals known to pose a risk. The World Cup in South Africa will doubtless show us this summer just what fun the stadium can be ...

SELECT BIBLIOGRAPHY

Adorno, Theodor W., *Prismen: Kulturkritik und Gesellschaft*, Berlin: Suhrkamp, 1955

——and Max Horkheimer, *Dialectic of Enlightenment*, trans. John Cumming London:Verso, 1997

——and Max Horkheimer, *Dialectic of Enlightenment: Philosophical Framgents*, ed. Gunzelin Schmidd Noerr, trans. Edmund Jephcott, Stanford: Stanford University Press, 2002

Baudrillard, Jean, 'Xerox and Infinity', in *The Transparency of Evil: Essays on Extreme Phenomena*, trans. James Benedict, London: Verso, 1993

Benjamin, Walter, 'The Work of Art in the Age of its Technological Reproducibility', in *The Work of Art in the Age of its Technological Reproducibility and Other Writings on Media*, ed. and trans. Michael William Jennings and Brigid Doherty, Cambridge, MA: Harvard University Press, 2008

Bergson, Henri, *Matter and Memory*, trans. Nancy Margaret Paul and W. Scott Palmer, New York: Zone Books, 1991

Brohm, Jean-Marie, *Critiques du sport*, Paris: Christian Bourgois, 1976

Diderot, Denis, 'Disconnected Thoughts on Painting, Sculpture and Poetry', trans. Kate Tunstall, in *Art in Theory, 1648–1815: An Anthology of Changing Ideas*, ed. Charles Harrison and Paul Wood, Oxford: Blackwell, 2000

Ellul, Jacques, *The Technological Society*, trans. John Wilkinson, New York: Knopf, 1964

Escriva, Jean-Pierre Escriva and Henri Vaugrand (eds), *L'Opium* sportif: *La critique radicale du sport, de l'extrème gauche à* Quel corps?, Paris: L'Harmattan, 1996

Hobsbawm, Eric, *The Age of Extremes: A History of the World, 1914– 1991*, New York: Pantheon, 1994

——*Nations and Nationalism since 1780: Programme, Myth, Reality*, Cambridge: Cambridge University Press, 1990

Jankélévitch, Vladimir, 'Une monstrueuse apothéose', in *Quel corps?* 6 (1976), reprinted in *Quel corps?*, Montreuil: Éditions de la Passion, 1986

Kracauer, Siegfried, 'Les Actualités cinématographiques', in *Le Voyage et la danse*, Paris: Éditions de la Maison des sciences de l'homme, 2008

Mandel, Ernest, *Marxist Economic Theory*, trans. Brian Pearce, London: Merlin, 1968

Marcuse, Herbert, *The Aesthetic Dimension: Toward a Critique of Marxist Aesthetics*, Boston: Beacon, 1977